A Few Honest Words

A Few Honest Words

The Kentucky Roots of Popular Music

Jason Howard

Foreword by Rodney Crowell

UNIVERSITY PRESS OF KENTUCKY

Scholarly publisher for the Commonwealth,
serving Bellarmine University, Berea College, Centre
College of Kentucky, Eastern Kentucky University,
The Filson Historical Society, Georgetown College,
Kentucky Historical Society, Kentucky State University,
Morehead State University, Murray State University,
Northern Kentucky University, Transylvania University,
University of Kentucky, University of Louisville,
and Western Kentucky University.
All rights reserved.

Editorial and Sales Offices: The University Press of Kentucky
663 South Limestone Street, Lexington, Kentucky 40508-4008
www.kentuckypress.com

16 15 14 13 12   5 4 3 2 1

Library of Congress Cataloging-in-Publication Data

Howard, Jason, 1981-
  A few honest words : the Kentucky roots of popular music / Jason Howard.
      pages ;   cm.
  Includes bibliographical references and index.
  ISBN 978-0-8131-3645-5 (hardcover : alk. paper) —
  ISBN 978-0-8131-3682-0 (pdf) — ISBN 978-0-8131-4059-9 (epub)
  1. Popular music—Kentucky—History and criticism. 2. Musicians—
Kentucky—Biography. I. Title.
  ML3477.7.K4H78 2012
  781.6409769—dc23
                              2012018998

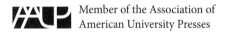

For Silas

We too would take up arms, the arms of our generation, the electric guitar and the microphone.

—Patti Smith, *Just Kids*

Contents

Foreword

My father, J. W. Crowell, grew up in Western Kentucky, in the Blood River bottoms of Calloway County. An enigma and a savant, he impacted my musical career more than anyone I've known. Although he had limited access to popular music—listening to the *Grand Ole Opry* on a neighbor's radio, going to local barn dances, or hearing his father play music on the front porch—he possessed an uncanny knack for learning songs. As a bandleader, his ability to absorb a song's essence in one or two listens and to keep a dance floor full was something to behold. He knew more songs than anyone I've ever met, from Appalachian dead-baby songs, to blues, to gospel songs, to songs about cocaine and murder and trains and jailhouses and sainted mothers. In later years, I called him the "human radio."

Musicians, singers, and songwriters like my father who were raised up in the South—particularly in the predominantly Scotch-Irish Appalachian region—defined what we know as the "high lonesome" sound. That tonality essentially defined country music in the first half of the twentieth century.

With each generation, roots music retains its appeal for the simple reason that the beautiful vulnerability that defines the human experience is best conveyed through song. Especially a well-written folk song.

In *A Few Honest Words,* you will learn how well-known artists such as Dwight Yoakam, Naomi Judd, Matraca Berg, and Joan Osborne are keeping that storied tradition alive. But you will also find that Kentucky's up-and-comers have a firm grip on their singular artistic vision.

By shining a light on an inclusive array of homegrown performing artists—some well known, some destined to be, and all of whom are in their own way following in the footsteps of Bill Monroe, Lionel Hampton, the Everly Brothers, and Loretta Lynn—Jason Howard has crafted a thoughtful and loving homage to his beloved state of Kentucky, giving us pitch-perfect journalistic prose from the heart of the country.

—Rodney Crowell

Introduction

My education in roots music began in front of an RCA turntable. One of my earliest memories is of my father guiding my hand to the arm of the record player, carefully moving the needle to the appropriate groove in the vinyl. I can still hear the crackle from the speakers, an intoxicating, rapid succession of pops and hisses, layered behind my father's voice: "That's how you do it."

And then the music—a shuffle rhythm, the strum of a guitar, a rolling banjo, and the voice of Loretta Lynn beckoning, "Just come on home to your blue Kentucky girl." Hers was a voice I had heard all of my six years, an accent on the tongues of every woman around me in Dorton Branch, a small holler in southeastern Kentucky.

My time at the turntable became a ritual I performed with devotion throughout my childhood, a secular religion spent kneeling on our orange shag carpet, thumbing through records by the Beatles, Ray Charles, and Johnny Cash. Although I did not yet have the vocabulary to articulate it, I sensed that I had been baptized in the river of roots music, submerged at the confluence of country, blues, rock, and gospel.

If there is a creed that defines roots music, it is that it consists of "three chords and the truth," an observation made by legendary songwriter and Kentuckian Harlan Howard. Although Howard was referring to country music, this definition can also extend to other genres.

Kentucky has historically been fertile ground for roots music. In music industry circles, musicians from Kentucky have long been acknowledged to possess an enviable pedigree—a lineage as prized as the bloodlines of the state's famous Thoroughbreds. Indeed, according to noted country music historian Charles Wolfe, "no other state had as much national attention lavished on its folk music."[1]

Although considerable historical scholarship has been devoted to Kentucky music, the majority of it has focused on three genres—folk, country, and bluegrass—at the expense of other styles. This fact, coupled with the growing popularity of the all-inclusive Americana genre, highlights the need for a redefinition of Kentucky music. Roots music in the Bluegrass State is more than just the hallowed mandolin of Bill Monroe and the banjo of the Osborne Brothers. It also includes the throbbing cello of Ben Sollee, the velvet crooning of jazz great Helen Humes, and the famed vibraphone of Lionel Hampton. It embraces rock, blues, jazz, gospel, and rap. It acknowledges diversity.

The musicians profiled in this book are included under this great umbrella. And like their musical ancestors, they are introducing the styles and sounds of Kentucky to the wider world, adding page after page to the state's expansive legacy in the Americana songbook. If you listen closely, you can hear Kentucky in their musical genes: Dwight Yoakam suggesting the mournful tones of Roscoe Holcomb, Nappy Roots channeling Blind Teddy Darby over a booming bass line, Ben Sollee and Daniel Martin Moore evoking the tight harmonies of the Everly Brothers. They represent all genres of roots music—country, blues, folk, jazz, rock, bluegrass, gospel, and rap. Some are household names. Others are emerging artists in their field. And two are local musicians who have simply played music all their lives in churches, coffeehouses, or neighborhood bars. They hail from all regions of the state.

My definition of a Kentuckian is fluid—I recognize Kentucky more as a spiritual state of mind than merely a physical place of birth. Many of these artists have migrated elsewhere—Nashville, New York, Los Angeles, Boston—to pursue their careers, but not a few have chosen to maintain a home base in Kentucky. One has never lived in Kentucky at all but identifies herself as a Kentuckian because of her mother's stories and lengthy summer visits to her grandparents' homeplace, a testament to the way the state can take up residence under one's skin. All, however, have been affected by the landscape, culture, and traditions of Kentucky, and this is reflected in their music.

I believe this to be Harlan Howard's truth—that "three chords" and a strong sense of place create the identifying mark of roots music. This truth echoes in the high, lonesome sounds of the Appalachians, in the gritty blues of Louisville, in the thumb-style guitar playing of the western coalfields. In the earthy soul of Joan Osborne, in the rich piano of Kevin Harris, in the ethereal guitar of My Morning Jacket's Jim James. It resides in the lyrics of the musicians profiled in this book—in the "beer can full of .22 holes" of Chris Knight, in "the slums / where we from" of Nappy Roots, in the "memory / knee deep in salvation" of Matraca Berg. It is at once rural and urban, black and white; it is country and blues and rock and folk and jazz and bluegrass and gospel and rap. It is one of us.

The Ballad Tradition

"It is generally believed that America has no folk-music, nothing distinctively native out of which a national school of advanced composition may arise," observed southern folklorist Emma Bell Miles in an article for *Harper's Magazine* in 1904. "But there is hidden among the mountains of Kentucky . . . a people of whose inner nature and musical expression almost nothing has been said."[2]

In retrospect, Miles's essay reads almost like an open invitation to scholars and musicologists, and indeed, a renowned British folk song collector named Cecil Sharp accepted her summons a dozen years later. Along with his colleague Maud Karpeles, Sharp spent nearly two years trekking across southern Appalachia in search of ballads and folk tunes. Much of their time was spent in Kentucky, visiting places such as the Hindman and Pine Mountain settlement schools, which were repositories of traditional music, according to folksinger Jean Ritchie: "If it hadn't been for the settlement schools," she observes, "many of the old mountain songs would have died out when the ways of the world came in on us."[3] Ritchie and her family had preserved many of the ballads the collectors were seeking. "Because we Ritchies loved to sing so well, we always listened to people singing songs we didn't know, and we caught many good ones that way," she recalls in her memoir *Singing Family of the Cumberlands.* "Some we learned from many different folks and without trying to, so when someone asks us, 'Where'd you learn that one?' we just can't say for sure. But with others we can name the very person that sang them to us."[4]

These collected songs appeared in print in 1932 as *English Folk Songs from the Southern Appalachians,* a volume containing 274 songs and ballads with 968 tunes, including "Sweet William" and "The Two Sisters." In the preface, Karpeles recounts that they "obtained the best ballad-texts" in Kentucky, "despite the intrusion of industrialism consequent on the finding of coal and oil."[5]

Although Sharp's collection was a boon for the international reputation of Kentucky music, it also served to perpetuate stereotypes of the state, which was depicted as an isolated locale where nearly everyone was a ballad singer. "In an ideal society," he proclaimed, "every child in his earliest years would as a matter of course develop this inborn capacity and learn to sing the songs of his forefathers . . . it was precisely this ideal state of things that I found existing in the mountain communities."[6]

Fellow ballad collector and Berea College professor James Watt Raine, while acknowledging that Appalachians had "suffered much from the misrepresentation of ignorant and superficial story writers," nonetheless echoed Sharp's view. "If George Washington could return," Raine mused, "he would not feel strange in these remote coves, so little have things changed since his day. Even Shakespeare would feel at home in these cabins."[7] But amid Raine's hyperbole lies significant insight: "The ballad is personal. It celebrates personal and individual adventures. One of us, one from our midst, suffered this sorrow, or endured this bitter wrong. The point of view is that of the common people."[8]

More recent historians have determined that the "common people" who sang these ballads were, in fact, a diverse sampling of the population—they were both male and female, rural and urban, black and white—a point that most early scholars, such as Sharp, purposefully overlooked. African American music historian Fred J. Hay offers a blunt criticism of Sharp's "narrow focus" on the supposedly pure Elizabethan tradition: "If not for his . . . lack of interest in African-American folk culture (and his apparent racism), Sharp would have undoubtedly recognized that the unique character of Appalachia ballad singing . . . which he identified as an independent invention of the good mountain folk was, in fact, learned through their contact with African Americans."[9]

In short, the music of Appalachia and, by extension, Kentucky is itself a metaphorical crazy quilt of roots genres, stitched together by people of varying ethnicities and backgrounds.

"Two Mighty Cultural Streams"

Mountaineers identified strongly with ballads and their themes of loss, hardship, and displacement. Some began composing their own tunes about people and events using these traditional songs as templates.[10] With the collapse of the coal industry following World War I, many Kentuckians were uprooted in search of employment. Although most took their songs with them, the inventions of the phonograph and the radio were largely responsible for bringing roots music to the masses.

The popularity of both hillbilly and race records, as they were labeled by the burgeoning music industry, soared. Newly created recording companies such as Victor and Columbia began setting up temporary studios in southern cities in search of talent. A Victor expedition to Bristol, Virginia, in August 1927 produced the first recordings of both the Carter Family and Jimmie Rodgers, a session that has often been described as the big bang of country music. The Bristol sessions also resulted in the recording of Kentucky gospel singers Alfred G. Karnes and Ernest Phipps.[11] Their journey to Bristol mirrored that of other Kentucky musicians, who were forced to travel long distances to reach these mobile studios because record companies often bypassed the state and focused their efforts in cities farther south.[12] One notable exception was a Victor session held in Louisville in June 1931, which featured cuts by the Carter Family and Jimmie Rodgers and, most significantly, included African American blues musicians such as the Louisville Jug Band, which served as Rodgers's band on "My Good Gal's Gone Blues," and guitarist Clifford "Grandpappy" Gibson, who accompanied Rodgers on "Let Me Be Your Side Track."[13] Gibson also recorded two solo cuts: "She Rolls It Slow" and "Railroad Man Blues."[14]

Despite record companies' focus on other southern states, many Kentucky musicians persevered to build successful recording careers. Hillbilly singers such as Buell Kazee and Doc Roberts were among the most popular recording artists of the 1920s and 1930s. While both were natives of Eastern Kentucky, their styles could not have been more different. Kazee's singing reflected his formal training, and he often appeared onstage in tie and tails.[15] Roberts, in contrast, developed a gritty fiddling technique that was influenced by musical exchanges with local black guitarists and fiddlers.[16]

This interracial musical pollination was widespread throughout the mountains, most famously with the joint travels of song catchers A. P. Carter (of Carter Family fame) and African American guitarist Lesley Riddle. The region, according to Hay, was becoming a repository for blues records, and Appalachians were listening to the latest songs of Blind Lemon Jefferson, Bessie Smith, and the Mississippi Sheiks, even co-opting the latter's "Sittin' on Top of the World" as a bluegrass standard.[17]

Historians have not adequately emphasized such interactions. Although Miles took note of a multicultural musical tradition in the mountains, her article for *Harper's* focused on "the tang of the Indian wilderness . . . mellowed by the English of Chaucer's time."[18] And Sharp ignored the blurring of musical traditions altogether, depicting mountain balladry and singing styles as purely Elizabethan in nature, a view that has since been refuted by most musicologists and historians. "If one looks for purity in the music of the South, one searches in vain," note Bill Malone and David Stricklin. "The folk music reservoir of the South was formed principally by the confluence of two mighty cultural streams, the British-Celtic and African."[19]

In the racially divided Jim Crow South, music became an acceptable arena of social contact between the two races through medicine shows, itinerant labor, and even integrated bands. "African Americans of Appalachia were . . . mobile," Hay observes. "They migrated—sometimes temporarily and sometimes permanently—to urban centers within the region; to Appalachian timber-harvesting, coal mining, and manufacturing areas; and outside the region to seek employment in northeastern and midwestern cities, as well as those of the southeast. Their music went with them."[20]

The legendary black string band Martin, Bogan, and Armstrong often visited the region's coal camps as part of a traveling medicine show. "They would be selling this fake medicine up there," Howard Armstrong recalled in 1990. "They'd meet a payday. They knew just when there was going to be a payday. And then we'd go up there and play and pass this bogus tonic and stuff on them."[21]

Music was the salvation of many itinerant workers, both black and white. Their manual labor on roads, on railroads, and in the mines often provided hard-won inspiration for their music, which they shared during their leisure hours. And despite the legal segregation of the time, integrated bands were not an uncommon sight, according to Armstrong. "Music was one medium where blacks and whites seemed to meet on very nice ground, common ground," he recalled. "Even in the small towns . . . and different places like that, they did integrate when it came to playing music."[22]

Perhaps the best example of this cross-racial pollination occurred in the coalfields of Western Kentucky in the early 1900s. There, an African American guitarist named Arnold Shultz developed what would turn out to be one of the most influential styles of instrumentation in any musical genre. According to Bill Monroe's biographer Richard D. Smith, if Shultz had been recorded, he "would today share the pantheon of African-American country blues greats with Mississippi John Hurt, Son House, and even Robert Johnson."[23] Even Wolfe—whose book *Kentucky Country* largely ignores African Americans' influence on country music in the state—was compelled to acknowledge Shultz, whose "distinct finger-picking style . . . involved picking out the lead and using the thumb to generate his own rhythm."[24]

Shultz played with several white string bands and other Kentucky musicians, and he even gave a young Bill Monroe his first paying gig.[25] In the process, he spawned a musical lineage that reads like the first chapter of the Gospel of Saint Matthew. His style begat that of guitarist Kennedy Jones, who in turn influenced guitarists Mose Rager and Ike Everly, who had formed a white string band in the area. Both Rager and Everly then passed the style on to celebrated country singer-songwriter Merle Travis, with whom it has become most identified under the sobriquet "Travis picking," and it is featured on songs such as "Dark as a Dungeon" and "Sixteen Tons." Everly's sons Don and Phil, better known as the Everly Brothers, introduced the technique to the world at large on their album *Songs Our Daddy Taught Us,* released at the height of their fame in 1958. Today, Shultz's technique, along with Maybelle Carter's famous "Carter scratch," has become one of the cornerstones of both popular and folk music.[26]

Working-Class Roots

Sales of both hillbilly and race records plummeted as the Great Depression swept the nation at the end of the 1920s.[27] At the same time, the popularity of radios soared, with fourteen million sets owned by 1930.[28] Americans were recognizing this new technology as a cheap, in-house form of entertainment. "Radio is my ticket to the World," Mrs. M. L. Higgins of Hopkinsville, Kentucky, wrote to *Rural Radio* magazine. "Our family vote the Radio the greatest paying investment we have ever made."[29]

People across the country shared Mrs. Higgins's sentiments and began tuning in to programs such as the great barn dances on WLS Chicago, WLW Cincinnati, and WWVA Wheeling and the Grand Ole Opry on WSM Nashville. Popular hillbilly music personalities emerged, many of whom were from Kentucky. Singers such as Bradley Kincaid, Red Foley, and Doc Roberts brought the musical traditions of their native state into the homes of displaced Kentuckians scattered across the country. And in a time of economic uncertainty, the sounds of home soothed the frayed nerves of these radio listeners. They, in turn, felt a deep need to share their stories with these singers, whom they identified as their own. "To my great surprise I found that you are a Kentuckian," Charles S. Matson of Los Angeles wrote to Roberts. "I was born at Hustonville in Lincoln County about forty years ago."[30]

Much of this identification was rooted in geography. Listeners recognized the images of farm life in the songs of Red Foley and Blind Teddy Darby and the urban sounds of Louisville in the music of Helen Humes and Lionel Hampton. But perhaps most important, they also responded to roots music because it "truly represented the organic evolution of the southern working class."[31] The influence of class on southern roots music has been well documented by historians and musicologists, particularly Bill Malone. In his book *Don't Get Above Your Raisin'*, Malone writes, "Neither southern folk culture nor southern folk music, therefore, can be understood apart from the story of industrialization."[32] The music that came out of the coal camps in both Eastern and Western Kentucky illustrates this point.

Members of the famed Garland family, a group of hell-raising Eastern Kentuckians that included Aunt Molly Jackson and her half siblings Sarah Ogun Gunning and Jim Garland, expressed in song the anger and frustration felt by many mining families in the region who were fighting for unionization during the 1930s. Compositions such as Jackson's "Ragged Hungry Blues" and "Hard Times in Coleman's Mines," along with Gunning's "Come All You Coal Miners" and Garland's "Death of Harry Simms," served as emblems of worker solidarity against the exploitations of the mining industry.

The coal mining experience was more subtly echoed in the western part of the state some two decades later in Merle Travis's celebrated "Sixteen Tons." Travis had been greatly affected by a hushed conversation he overheard among his father and other union miners about the struggle in Harlan County, as well as by life in the hardscrabble Beech Creek mines in his own Muhlenberg County. The song title refers to a tradition carried out on a young miner's first day on the job, when the older miners would reduce their output to allow the trainee to load sixteen tons. "It was a sign of manhood to be initiated by reaching this excessive figure," according to folk music historian Archie Green.[33]

The labor-oriented legacy of musicians such as Jackson and Travis has persisted and even expanded, with subsequent songs evoking a sense of outrage about the devastation of Kentucky's topography. Eastern Kentucky native Jean Ritchie famously declared her desire to "buy Perry County and run them all out" in her song "Black Waters," a protest against the coal industry that was written in the 1960s. A decade later, John Prine penned "Paradise," which is arguably his masterpiece. In it, he mourns the destruction of Muhlenberg County, where "Mr. Peabody's coal train done hauled it away." More recently, the Reel World String Band has produced songs such as "Cranks Creek," which recounts the collapse of a coal waste impoundment in Harlan County.

But images of Kentucky's working class have not been restricted to labor and protest songs. They have also influenced gospel music across the state, most notably in the work of Dottie Rambo, who, as a nine-year-old, began writing songs on a creek bank in her native Western Kentucky.[34] She went on to compose songs "sparked with crisp, clear, concrete images drawn from her rural background and southern life," in the words of Wolfe.[35] In "The Holy Hills of Heaven Call Me," one of her finest songs, Rambo combines the rolling topography of the region with more traditional scenes of mansions and starry crowns in an apparent desire to escape the laborious hardships of an earthly life.

Images of rural Kentucky have even begun to penetrate rap music, which is widely seen as an urban genre. Nappy Roots, one of rap's most successful groups, was formed on the campus of Western Kentucky University in Bowling Green in the mid-1990s. Included on the group's first album, *Watermelon, Chicken & Gritz*, is a song titled "Kentucky Mud": "Country living, and the country cookin' in a country kitchen / Good intention and strong religion, it's a strong tradition." Songs such as these, rooted in class struggles and a rural sense of place, have reached a wide swath of Americans by following the time-tested rule that the specific is, in fact, universal. Images such as front porches, country kitchens, railroads, coal mining fathers, moonshining, square dances, and redbud trees have become a shorthand way of identifying the singer as "one of us."

Roots music historians consistently point to Tom T. Hall as an example of someone who not only incorporates these traditional images into his music but also is inspired by his fellow Kentuckians. Songs such as "The Year that Clayton Delaney Died" and "A Week in a Country Jail" were written directly from personal experience. "I was trying to put the way I felt about this country and these people into words," Hall recounts in his memoir *The Storyteller's Nashville*. "The thing that fascinated me the most during my childhood were the people that I grew up with. I was awed by these people, and I admired them and feared them. I was also one of them."[36]

Kentucky Women

Recent historians have emphasized the changing roles of women in both southern and Kentucky roots music. Wolfe chronicles this evolution in his book *Kentucky Country*, and the subject inspired an excellent account by country music historians Mary A. Bufwack and Robert K. Oermann titled *Finding Her Voice: The Saga of Women in Country Music*. Both books observe that by the late 1930s, women had become a permanent fixture in country music. Radio listeners across the country were well acquainted with the voices of Sara and Maybelle Carter, Patsy Montana, and Linda Parker. Yet most female performers were objectified with the label "girl singers"—mere novelty acts in a male-dominated industry.

In her 1980 autobiography, musician Lily May Ledford recounts how she formed one of the first all-female string bands under the direction of radio personality and entrepreneur John Lair. "We got the bright idea of naming ourselves *The Wild Wood Flowers*. Straight we went to Mr. Lair and asked him if we could do this. He was kind and tactful, but laughed a little and said, 'Girls, I had thought a more country name would be best. How about *Coon Creek Girls*?'"[37] Ledford had no say in the name of her band or in her onstage appearance: "In the long old-fashioned dress and high-top lace up shoes that Mr. Lair had me wear, I felt like an old lady and not at all pretty. Mr. Lair discouraged my buying clothes, curling my hair, going in for make-up or improving my English. 'Stay a mountain girl, just like you were when you came here. Be genuine and plain at all times,' he said. I did so want to look like the others and did a little fixing up in spite of him and would not wear my hair pulled back in a bun except on stage."[38]

Although Ledford and the Coon Creek Girls were largely created for the barn dance radio shows, their uniqueness as an all-female band—along with their considerable musical abilities—set them apart. "When the Coon Creek Girls . . . and their high mountain harmony burst on the scene," Wolfe observes, "ears perked and heads turned. Here were no sentimental parlor songs about mother, and no Tin Pan Alley odes to prairie sweethearts. Here was mountain music coming in the front door."[39] The Coon Creek Girls were so popular that first lady Eleanor Roosevelt requested that they play at the White House for King George VI and Queen Elizabeth in 1939.

Ledford was never able to stand up to Lair, an ambitious businessman who worked for WLS Chicago and WLW Cincinnati and eventually created the Renfro Valley Barn Dance. But he more than met his match in a singer from Western Kentucky named Cynthia May Carver, better known as Cousin Emmy. A platinum blonde who could play nearly any instrument, Emmy was "part carnival barker and part mountain folk song preserver, part medicine show huckster and part sincere sentimentalist," write Bufwack and Oermann. "She was innocent and brash, yet shrewd and savvy. Emmy's formal schooling reportedly consisted of just two weeks, and she learned to read by poring over mail-order catalogs, but she was as sharp and canny as any business college grad."[40]

In an extraordinary letter to Lair after a disheartening radio experience in Knoxville, Tennessee, Emmy proposed a partnership: "Mr. Lair I will cut you in any way you see fit," reads her awkward cursive. "Now is our chance to make some money."[41] Lair declined Emmy's offer, but she was undeterred and became "country music's first independent, unmarried, self-supporting female touring attraction."[42] Emmy even took her act to the silver screen, appearing in films such as *Swing in the Saddle* and *The Second Greatest Sex* alongside B-movie legend Mamie Van Doren. After lapsing into semiobscurity in the late 1950s, Emmy was coaxed out of retirement a decade later by the New Lost City Ramblers and enjoyed a career resurgence due to the folk music revival.

Around this time, Helen Humes was charting her own course in the world of jazz. Born and raised in Louisville, she learned to play the trumpet and piano and sang in the Sunday school band. She made her first recording in 1927 in St. Louis, at the age of fourteen, and she was soon singing with orchestras in New York. After recording with Harry James in 1937, she turned down a job with the legendary Count Basie because the pay was too low. Humes had second thoughts, however, and accepted the offer the following year, replacing none other than Billie Holiday. The silkiness of her voice salvaged much of the inferior material she was given, and it shone on the better songs. The mid-1940s found Humes working alone on the West Coast and moving into rhythm and blues, scoring the hits "Be-Baba-Leba" and "Million Dollar Secret" in the process. Although her career slowed in the 1960s, it was reignited by a reunion with Count Basie at the 1973 Newport Folk Festival and continued until her death in 1981.[43]

Loretta Lynn, arguably Kentucky's most recognizable musician, has been accorded the most attention by historians. As the self-professed "Coal Miner's Daughter," Lynn and her music have always served as the intersection of class and gender. She "set the standard" for songs about working people, according to Malone, and incorporated rural imagery—much of it from her Kentucky childhood—into her music.[44] Indeed, "she was unable to escape the influence of the land and what it represented."[45] But Lynn also symbolized her own hard-hitting brand of feminism, from warning her man ("Don't Come Home a Drinkin' [with Lovin' on Your Mind]") to trumpeting the benefits of birth control ("The Pill"). In the words of Roy Blount Jr.: "Listen, Loretta was out kicking ass when Gloria Steinem was wearing a Bunny suit for an article in *Show*."[46] "By no means was Loretta the first country singer to sing from a woman's point of view," Wolfe explains, "but her songs were by far the most popular, and the most successful of them. Their success reflected an important trend in country music: the emergence of a large female audience."[47]

Back to the River

We are in the midst of a roots music renaissance, as people across the country are returning to a music of place. They are rejecting the glossy ad campaigns, images, and sounds that accompany the latest Nashville sensations, opting instead for comfort food for the ears. Just like chicken and dumplings, mashed potatoes, and a pone of cornbread served up on your mama's dinner table, many Americans in urban and rural areas alike are longing for a return to the basics: a guitar, evocative lyrics, and a voice that has not been autotuned or tampered with in Pro Tools.

The Americana radio format is booming, and many of the musicians profiled in this book are leading the way. Artists as diverse as Patty Griffin, with her soulful brand of folk music; Calexico, with their Latin-flavored country rock; and the Carolina Chocolate Drops, one of the last all–African American string bands, are being embraced. Roots music festivals are cropping up across the country, most notably the Americana Music Festival and Conference held in Nashville each year and featuring four days of musical showcases from some of the genre's most popular artists, capped by a star-studded awards ceremony at the Ryman Auditorium.

No Depression, a quarterly magazine founded in the mid-1990s and named for the old Carter Family tune, has morphed from a print publication into an online presence, introducing Americana music to fans around the world through features, blog posts, and album and live concert reviews. Even the National Academy of Recording Arts and Sciences has taken notice of the genre's growth, adding a category for Best Americana Album to the Grammy Awards. In November 2011 the Public Broadcasting System aired a special titled *ACL Presents: Americana Music Festival,* filmed during the sold-out 2011 Americana Music Association's honors and awards ceremony in Nashville. "Americana as a community is growing," stated the association's executive director, Jed Hilly, in remarks at the ceremony. "I believe it holds the keys for the success and resurgence of the music business on the whole. This is because it is artist driven and artist supported. Earlier this year, during the weeks before and after the Grammys, Americana had five albums in *Billboard*'s Top 15 Album chart—all genres. This summer Merriam Webster entered the word *Americana* into its most discerning dictionary. The landscape is changing and we, the Americana community, are changing it."

Like so many others, I strayed from the sanctuary of roots music during my teenage and college years, following the fun but ultimately false pop idols of the late 1990s. I returned to the fold one spring afternoon in 2003 at a listening station at Melody Record Shop in the heart of Dupont Circle in Washington, D.C., surrounded by rows upon rows of CDs and sacred vinyl. If our lives can be chronicled by the albums we listen to and the iTunes playlists we create, then this encounter with Rosanne Cash's *Rules of Travel* was my musical Road to Damascus moment. As soon as I heard the hypnotic keyboards of the title track, followed by that piercing electric guitar hook, I repented on the spot, her sinuous voice absolving me of my transgressions. I carried the album to the cash register, shared a laugh with the manager, and walked out onto Connecticut Avenue reborn, retracing my steps back to the Metro, back to the record player of my childhood. Back to the truth.

Notes

1. Charles K. Wolfe, *Kentucky Country: Folk and Country Music of Kentucky* (Lexington: University Press of Kentucky, 2009), 4, 5.

2. Emma Bell Miles, "Some Real American Music," *Harper's Magazine,* June 1904, 118.

3. Quoted in Mary A. Bufwack and Robert K. Oermann, *Finding Her Voice: The Saga of Women in Country Music* (New York: Crown, 1993), 5.

4. Jean Ritchie, *Singing Family of the Cumberlands* (Lexington: University Press of Kentucky, 1988), 128–29.

5. Cecil Sharp, *English Folk Songs from the Southern Appalachians* (London: Oxford University Press, 1932), xv.

6. Ibid., xxv.

7. James Watt Raine, "The Way of Life of the Mountain People of Appalachia" (unpublished), 1, 2C–3, Berea College Appalachian Sound Archives.

8. James Watt Raine, lecture notes, Berea College Appalachian Sound Archives.

9. Fred J. Hay, "Black Musicians in Appalachia: An Introduction to Affrilachian Music," *Black Music Research Journal* 23, no. 1–2 (2003): 7–8.

10. Wolfe, *Kentucky Country,* 8.

11. Ibid., 38.

12. Ibid., 26.

13. Lawrence Cohn et al., *Nothing But the Blues: The Music and the Musicians* (New York: Abbeville Press, 1999), 251.

14. Vladimir Bogdanov, *All Music Guide to the Blues: The Definitive Guide to the Blues* (Montclair, NJ: Backbeat Books, 2003), 202.

15. Wolfe, *Kentucky Country,* 32–34.

16. Ibid., 29.

17. Hay, "Black Musicians in Appalachia," 7.

18. Miles, "Some Real American Music," 123.

19. Bill C. Malone and David Stricklin, *Southern Music/American Music* (Lexington: University Press of Kentucky, 2003), 5.

20. Hay, "Black Musicians in Appalachia," 16.

21. Quoted in Barry Lee Pearson, "Appalachian Blues," *Black Music Research Journal* 23, no. 1–2 (2003): 38.

22. Ibid., 46–47.

23. Richard D. Smith, *Can't You Hear Me Callin': The Life of Bill Monroe, Father of Bluegrass* (Cambridge: Da Capo Press, 2001), 23.

24. Wolfe, *Kentucky Country*, 113.

25. Smith, *Can't You Hear Me Callin'*, 24.

26. Wolfe, *Kentucky Country*, 112–18.

27. Malone and Stricklin, *Southern Music/American Music*, 71.

28. Wolfe, *Kentucky Country*, 46.

29. Letter from Mrs. M. L. Higgins to *Rural Radio* 1, no. 4 (May 1938): 2.

30. Letter from Charles S. Matson to Doc Roberts, 6 June 1927, Doc Roberts Papers, Berea College Appalachian Sound Archives.

31. Bill Malone, *Don't Get Above Your Raisin': Country Music and the Southern Working Class* (Urbana: University of Illinois Press, 2002), 16.

32. Ibid., 24.

33. Archie Green, *Only a Miner: Studies in Recorded Coal-Mining Songs* (Urbana: University of Illinois Press, 1972), 311–12, 360–61.

34. Bufwack and Oermann, *Finding Her Voice*, 207.

35. Wolfe, *Kentucky Country*, 148.

36. Tom T. Hall, *The Storyteller's Nashville* (New York: Doubleday, 1979), 170, 171.

37. Lily May Ledford, *Coon Creek Girl* (Berea, KY: Berea College Appalachian Center, 1980), 20.

38. Ibid.

39. Wolfe, *Kentucky Country*, 81.

40. Bufwack and Oermann, *Finding Her Voice*, 100.

41. Letter from Cousin Emmy to John Lair, 11 February 1941, Berea College Appalachian Sound Archives.

42. Bufwack and Oermann, *Finding Her Voice*, 101.

43. "Helen Humes, a Voice with Style," African American Registry, http://www.aaregistry.org/historic_events/view/helen-humes-voice-style.

44. Malone, *Don't Get Above Your Raisin'*, 48.

45. Wolfe, *Kentucky Country*, 162.

46. Roy Blount, "Country's Angels," *Esquire* 87, no. 3 (March 1977).

47. Wolfe, *Kentucky Country*, 165.

1

Naomi Judd

Ancestral Memory

Naomi Judd knows her way around the kitchen. She moves from drawer to cabinet to refrigerator without missing a beat, handing out tall glasses of sweet tea. *Grace* is a word that comes to mind as she performs this southern ritual. Her kitchen dance is fluid and familiar, reminiscent of her days onstage with her daughter Wynonna as the Judds, one of the most successful duos in country music history.

But instead of sporting her trademark red vinyl party dress—the one with the industrial-strength crinolines that now resides in the Country Music Hall of Fame—she wears a simple white shirt and navy blue cotton pants. Her wine-colored hair is pulled back and tied at the nape of her neck. And, most extraordinarily, she is sans makeup, her ivory skin luminescent in the Tennessee summer sunlight that peers through the kitchen windows. She turns her attention to the saucepan simmering on the island stovetop, then looks up and grins. "It's rattlesnake pasta today, boys," she growls. "With a bite."

Naomi talks of literature, science, and her native Kentucky as she stirs the pasta and lifts up a lid to check on the steaming broccoli. Satisfied with its progress, she whips around and opens a large, deep drawer. I recognize it with one glance and suppress a smile—it's her kitchen medicine cabinet. Every Appalachian woman I know has one.

She rummages for the appropriate bottle. In her former life—the one before the fourteen number-one hits and six Grammy Awards and twenty million records sold—she was a nurse at the nearby Williamson County Hospital in Franklin. It's easy to imagine her in starched whites and rubber-soled shoes as she counts out pills with deft precision before disappearing into the adjoining dining room.

Naomi returns to serve the food, and we carry our plates and glasses through the door to the antique dining table. I pause and take in the room. We are surrounded on all sides by overflowing bookshelves: medical tomes by Andrew Weil and Francis Collins, Appalachian literature by Lee Smith and Silas House, spiritual works by Archbishop Desmond Tutu and Bill Moyers.

"We like to eat in the library," she laughs.

We take our seats, and she motions us to join hands for an extraordinary grace, straight out of the gospel according to Walt Whitman:

> Why should I wish to see God better than this day?
> I see something of God each hour of the twenty-four, and
>   each moment then,
> In the faces of men and women I see God, and in my own
>   face in the glass,
> I find letters from God dropt in the street, and every one is
>   sign'd by God's name
> And I leave them where they are, for I know that
>   wheresoe'er I go,
> Others will punctually come for ever and ever.

"Amen," we all offer in unison, and reach for our silverware.

Naomi Judd. (Photo courtesy of artist's management)

She stops us, calling attention to the two pills from her Appalachian pharmacy that she has placed above our plates. "Take your vitamins."

"I feel like it's the greatest blessing I've ever had to be an Appalachian," Naomi says, staring at a blue jay outside the window of her great room. She is curled up in her favorite chair, her legs covered by a throw. "If you remember who you are, nobody can take that from you. Your memories are associated through the land." She pauses, still watching the bird. Then another word, a whisper, as she turns to look me dead in the eye: "sacred."

Appalachia has always been hallowed ground to Naomi Judd. A seventh-generation Kentuckian, she was born Diana Ellen Judd on 11 January 1946 in Ashland, in the northeastern part of the state, and was raised in a house that her parents, Charles Glen and

Pauline, purchased from her paternal grandparents when she was four.

"This house—this big old four-square that looked like *The Waltons'* house—was just like a womb to me," she recalls. "I remember very clearly going into that house with [my grandparents] Ogden and Sally Ellen Judd, and Uncle Milt sitting in his chair, listening to the Cincinnati Reds and spitting tobacco in his Maxwell House coffee can. And Aunt Pauline, who lived up in the attic when she came to town."

These family members resided upstairs, along with the occasional renter, while Diana lived downstairs with her parents and three younger siblings, Brian, Mark, and Margaret. "We were so connected," she says.

Despite this closeness, she explains that theirs was not an environment that fostered creativity. "I heard no music when I was growing up. When we got a TV, it was the first art, if you will, that was ever brought into our experience. We were the most unmusical, uncreative family. Movies and TV were my music."

Instead, Diana's imagination was developed outside of Ashland—at the family's homeplace in nearby Louisa, which was run by her great-aunts Zora and Margie.

"I grew up with this dynastic awareness of the land. It was just as much a part of me as these blood relatives. I knew how to differentiate a nonpoisonous snake from a poisonous snake. I knew that you planted marigolds and zinnias around your garden to throw off those that would eat the seeds. I knew what it was like to pull a root vegetable out of the ground, brush the dirt off, draw the water from the well, and then wash and eat it. When it would come time to go home, I'd almost want to hide because I didn't want to go back to town."

When she wasn't in school in Ashland, Diana would often pass time at her father's small Art Deco filling station, drinking

Nehi Grape, playing pinball, and listening to the loafers talk as they chain-smoked unfiltered Camel cigarettes. She would use her allowance to see movies at the Paramount and Capitol theaters, or she would simply be outdoors—walking to the library or playing with her pets.

Hers was an idyllic childhood, one that is often conjured by reflecting on small-town America in the 1950s. A gauzy black-and-white movie before the reality of Technicolor: "I was a very obedient kid. I was one of these little girls who made all As and kept my room clean and played piano at the First Baptist Church. But in 1963, the world as I knew it blew up."

That year, her brother Brian was diagnosed with Hodgkin's disease. And the night before she started her senior year in high school, Diana became pregnant.

"He left town, and we never heard from him again," she says of the father.

She quickly married Michael Ciminella—a local boy she had been dating—and set up housekeeping in his parents' home. Christina (who later became Wynonna) arrived soon after and took the Ciminella name. After Michael enrolled at the University of Kentucky, Diana and her new family moved to Lexington.

She had a difficult time adjusting to apartment life and spent her time caring for Christina, missing Ashland, and worrying about Brian.

"I was always different, my mom will tell you. I would see people when I was growing up that weren't accepted and were in some sort of pain, and my empathy could not be quenched. And nobody else in my family was demonstrative when Brian died."

A long silence falls. Naomi begins to rearrange the fringes on her throw, placing the strings precisely, fanning them out in perfect arches. It's obvious that nearly fifty years after her brother's untimely death at age seventeen, Naomi's sorrow still lingers, and it fills the room.

"Dr. Franz came to the house and gave everybody a little red pill, and we were all sent to our bedrooms. Nobody talked about it from that day on."

Although it wasn't discussed, Brian Judd's death was a watershed moment for Naomi's family, one that took her years of reflection to recognize. "It caused my Mom and Dad's divorce; my brother became a preacher, my sister left town and sort of turned her back on our roots, I became a nurse, Brian's best friend became a pediatrician."

But in the meantime, Diana returned to Lexington. Upon Michael's graduation, the family moved to Los Angeles, where Diana gave birth to daughter Ashley in April 1968. Three years later, Diana and Michael separated, and they divorced the following year. She became a single mother, raising Christina and Ashley just off the Sunset Strip in West Hollywood. It was there, in the wake of her broken marriage and bouts of homesickness, that she began to discover the meaning of her Kentucky heritage.

"It was painful," she explains. "I didn't understand the concrete. I didn't understand the smog, the noise. It could not have been more radically extreme."

Diana's Eastern Kentucky accent often attracted attention: "People would always ask me to say *night* and *alright*. And the other word was *wash*. 'I'm gonna *warsh* my clothes.'" She rolls her eyes. "So I didn't tell people I knew how to make lye soap. They wouldn't care. It wouldn't mean anything to them. I didn't want to say that because I knew that would make me mad, that they didn't think that was important."

Despite this culture shock, Naomi admits that living in West Hollywood also made her "insatiably curious." She paid the rent and supported her daughters by working at a health food store, being a girl Friday, and taking the occasional modeling gig. One black-and-white photograph from her foray into modeling shows her in full makeup, her shoulders exposed dramatically in a 1940s-style striped dress, a cigarette dangling lustily from her lips. Looking at the picture, it's apparent that Diana could have had her choice of men. Her sensuous beauty is on full display, interwoven with a quiet intelligence and flamboyant style. She looks like a better version of Jaclyn Smith in her *Charlie's Angels* heyday.

So her next sentence comes as a complete surprise: "I fell in love with an ex-con on heroin who beat me and almost killed me one night." Bloodied and bruised, she took her daughters and checked into a nearby hotel, where she made a decision. "They had an APB out for him and a restraining order. I had to leave California to get away from him for my life. That's why I went to the mountaintop in Kentucky."

Morrill, Kentucky, lies eight miles southeast of Berea on U.S. Highway 421. A cluster of vinyl-sided houses along the main road forms the nucleus of the small community, which is tucked among trees dripping with kudzu. Graveled, one-lane offshoots lead to other homes farther back in the hills. It's an isolated mountain hamlet, a refuge where deer, farmers, and back-to-the-landers peacefully coexist.

To Diana, returning to Kentucky meant a chance for a new life. She enrolled in the nursing program at Eastern Kentucky University, hoping to eventually work for the Frontier Nursing Service in Hyden. After living in a primitive cabin along the Kentucky River, Diana rented "Chanticleer"—a rambling, two-story wood house in Morrill—from a Berea College music professor. Writing about it years later in her autobiography, *Love Can Build*

Naomi Judd's Theology

Naomi's spiritual journey is nearly as fascinating as her life story. "I always recognized God," she says of her childhood. "I'd be out in the woods at the farm and just talk to God. But I remember being completely unsatisfied with church."

Raised in a strict Baptist congregation, she remembers sitting in the pew every Sunday morning with her brother Brian, both of them waiting for the pastor to deliver his trademark action with his large red Bible. "At some point, he'd slam that thing on the pulpit three times," she says, leaning forward in her chair to act it out. "He'd say, 'God said it!'—BAM—'I believe it!'—BAM—'That settles it!'—BAM. And it made me angry."

Curious by nature, Naomi refused to accept such one-dimensional answers, and today her theology is an amalgam of faith and science. "Teach me about quantum physics, because that's when I really get into God," she laughs. "Neurotheology is about finding the place in the brain—it's called the 'God spot.' Our temporal lobes are the most mammalian, primal parts of our brain. They're instinctive. It's emotionality. The parietal lobe gives you your sense of self, that you're an individual. So when you do an MRI of the brain of a Buddhist monk or one of these nuns or a snake handler or someone who's meditating, the parietal lobe just shuts down. All the neurochemicals just cascade. And these are like red-hot. They're on fire."

Naomi lingers for a moment on that image before continuing. "In today's world, music lights up the right temporal lobe. . . . There's a neuroscientific reason why music takes us to our higher self and is a window to God. Music, right now, I think is more important than it's ever been."

a Bridge, Naomi remembered: "It was like an Appalachian museum. Furnished with hand-carved Vermont maple furniture, it was filled with antiques, large hand-braided rugs, heirloom quilts, a stone fireplace, and glory of glories, a Steinway grand piano!"

Just the mention of Chanticleer brings a smile to her face even now, nearly forty years later. "It was the perfect place after Hollywood. A tonic."

She became friends with a neighbor, the imposing Minnie Yancey, who was ten years older than Diana and a natural mentor. "She wore work boots, pioneer outfits, with long, black hair parted down the middle. A very robust woman." Naomi laughs at the memory. "She was a weaver. She had a loom that she built herself." Immediately captivated, Naomi remembers thinking about Minnie: "I like you better than the broads in LA who had plastic surgery and got their nails done and went to lunch with the girls."

Without the distractions of a TV or telephone, Diana and the girls subsisted on nature and words for entertainment. They spent the summer days picking blackberries, drying apples, and raising a garden. In the evenings, they sat on the porch, telling stories and singing songs.

"I gave Ashley *The Chronicles of Narnia,* and that's when her imagination blossomed. But then. . . ." Naomi grins and shakes her head, remembering the young Wynonna. "We couldn't talk to each other, but we could sing together. It's when I discovered music."

She bought Christina a secondhand guitar, and a neighbor, Craig Williams, began to teach her chords. One day while Diana was in Berea, she wandered into a music store on Main Street. Looking through the bargain bin, she came across an album by two women: Hazel Dickens and Alice Gerrard. She couldn't wait to get it back to Chanticleer.

"I heard these songs and it was like you were wearing the most beautiful outfit in the world that someone had made just for you. It was your color. It was your fabric. And frankly, my life had been so hardscrabble and so iffy that there was an amazing comfort in that music. The songs on that album were just perfect for us." Diana and Christina learned them in quick succession: "Custom Made Woman Blues," "Hello Stranger," "Miner's Blues," "The Sweetest Gift."

"I'd never thought about where songs come from," Naomi admits. Her interest was piqued, though, when she watched Minnie's daughter, Sonja, write a song. "It opened up the process." She began writing songs around the house, nothing more than ditties to pass the time and entertain the girls. I ask her to sing a couple of them, and she smoothes her hair, leans forward, and lets loose that husky alto, so rarely heard without Wynonna's piercing lead. A few lines of "Simple, Peaceful, and Good"—written on the front porch when a storm was rolling in—and the rollicking *chug-a-chug* chorus of "Soup Beans and Cornbread," a humorous tune about the unofficial food of Appalachia. And then she launches into one written especially for Christina:

> I don't use such a word as can't
> Now don't you tell me I'm crazy, I ain't
> When you're saying something can't be done
> Just look again, honey, I'll be the one

When she gets to the last line, she raises her right index finger, the same wag she used onstage when Wynonna would wail "Mama didn't raise no fool" just before the chorus of "Give a Little Love" came back around. It's a telling gesture, a nonverbal reminder that Naomi had felt the bite and scorn of that degrading word—*can't*—firsthand, having heard it countless times as a pregnant teenager, an unsatisfied housewife, a divorcée, a hillbilly expatriate in Hollywood, a single mother, a nontraditional college student.

Writers often say that the first rule of their craft is to "write what you know." Although composed for her daughter, "Can't" could just as easily have been Diana Ellen Judd's memoir.

By 1976, Diana had undergone so many incarnations that she felt like a different version of herself. Reinvigorated by her time in Kentucky, she decided to tackle California again and relocated to Marin County, just north of San Francisco. With this move, Diana decided to cast off an old appendage, one that she had carried around for thirty years: her name.

Her selection of *Naomi* was not random. It marked an intentional transformation, chosen in honor of a mentally challenged girl she remembered from Ashland. But her new appellation had biblical implications as well. In the book of Ruth, the character Naomi undergoes a profound metamorphosis. At the beginning of the story, she is an empty woman, battered and beaten down by life. By the book's conclusion, however, Naomi has been transformed to a state of wholeness. This change occurs when she establishes a firm sense of place based on her daughter-in-law Ruth's promise: "Entreat me not to leave thee: for whither thou goest, I will go; and where thou lodgest, I will lodge: thy people shall be my people, and thy God my God. So the two went until they came to Bethlehem." Despite her lack of an established physical home, Naomi's two years in Kentucky and the advent of roots music in her life created a fixed spiritual sense of place.

She enrolled in the nursing program at the College of Marin, gaining practical experience at a hospital in nearby Oakland and working nights as a waitress. Her meager wages were only enough for rent and food, so she turned to Aid to Families with Dependent Children to cover the girls' medical needs. In her few minutes of spare time, she and Christina began learning songs by Bonnie Raitt, Ella Fitzgerald, and the Boswell Sisters.

"I realized this was her gift," Naomi says of her older daughter. "Her destiny. She would never have had a nine-to-five gig." Christina sensed this as well and began to embrace a new identity of her own. Following her mother's lead, she changed her name to Wynonna, after a place name—albeit with a different spelling—in the song "Route 66."

They made their first demos, covering the Delmore Brothers' "Hillbilly Boogie," later adding the tracks "Kentucky" and "Let Me Be Your Baby." Turning their attention to live shows, they began performing at every opportunity, even singing backup for a local band called Susie and the Cowpokes. But it wasn't enough for the burgeoning duo. Upon receiving her nursing degree, Naomi sent Ashley back to Kentucky to live with her father, Michael, and Naomi and Wynonna set out for Nashville.

She wrote about this time of upheaval in her autobiography: "The general outcry from the folks back in Kentucky was: 'What in the world are you doing?' The Ciminellas and my folks were greatly disturbed by my bizarre scheme. . . . They called . . . all the time and the fear and outrage in their voices jumped out through the receiver."

Still, Naomi persevered. She and Wynonna arrived in Nashville in May 1979 and were disappointed when they found that it looked like every other city. After a stint working a dead-end job on Music Row and living in a grungy motel on Murfreesboro Pike, Naomi settled in an old farmhouse on Del Rio Pike in Franklin, a quaint town about twenty miles outside of Nashville.

"There was no insulation," she says. "I mean, you could literally see the dirt through the cracks of the floor."

She sent for Ashley, enrolled the girls in school, and took a job as a night nurse at Williamson County Hospital. But on her days off, she cultivated contacts in the music industry. "Part of me was feeling feisty, because by now I had figured out that I had this Hollywood knowledge."

Using her smooth talk and vivacious personality to full effect, Naomi landed their first break, a spot on the early-morning televised *Ralph Emery Show*. They were paid twenty-five dollars each and were ecstatic, despite the fact that Emery mangled their names. Frustrated, he dubbed them "the Soap Sisters" in subsequent appearances, after learning about Naomi's soap-making skills.

In spite of this exposure, it was a fateful on-the-job encounter that proved most beneficial to the musical future of Naomi and Wynonna. While working at the hospital, Naomi was assigned to care for Dianna Maher, a seventeen-year-old who had been seriously injured in a car accident. Dianna recognized Naomi from the *Ralph Emery Show* and mentioned that her father worked in the music industry and co-owned a recording studio. After Dianna was discharged, Naomi went to the studio and slipped Brent Maher a homemade tape of her original songs created on a thirty-dollar Kmart tape recorder. Six weeks later, Maher called. "I felt shot through with electricity," Naomi wrote in *Love Can Build a Bridge*. "Brent Maher was like water after a drought."

Maher began to visit the house on Del Rio Pike for practice sessions, often bringing musicians with him to provide the accompaniment. Then, through another chance encounter in June 1982, Naomi met Ken Stilts Sr., a well-connected businessman who owned a small record label and agreed to manage them. Stilts took their demo straight to the top, playing it for Joe Galante, the head of RCA, whose roster included such country music royalty as Dolly Parton, Ronnie Milsap, Kenny Rogers, and Alabama. Galante granted them a rare live audition in the RCA boardroom on 2 March 1983.

"I was wearing a flea market dress," Naomi says. "Wynonna and I weren't speaking to each other. I'd let her rabbit out in the field, and she would not even talk to me."

Moments before they entered the boardroom, Naomi began to feel the pressure. "You have to remember—I'm the mom and I was supposed to be the responsible adult. I had no earthly idea what I was doing. I went into the restroom stall at RCA, and I remember looking in that mirror and telling myself, 'Wait a minute. Think of all the things that you survived. You've been shot at. You've survived floods and fires and earthquakes, beaten up and everything. Go and sing.'"

Naomi left the bathroom, and she and Wynonna walked down the hallway to the boardroom. Squeezing her daughter's hand, she whispered, "We're back in Morrill. Let's just lock eyes."

It was that thought that quelled their nerves. As they sang "The Sweetest Gift," the old Hazel and Alice song they had learned years before in Morrill, Naomi and Wynonna were carried back to Kentucky, back to the mountaintop and the front porch of Chanticleer, back to Craig Williams and Minnie Yancey. Their soothing memories of Kentucky pulled them through.

Naomi and Wynonna were RCA recording artists.

Nearly thirty years after her official entry into country music, after all the platinum albums and awards and sold-out tours, it is the land that Naomi holds most dear. The solitude of her Peaceful Valley farm is a balm. Tucked away among the rolling hills of Leipers Fork, just outside of Franklin, it recalls the landscape of her beloved Morrill. As she moves among the poplars and pines, it's evident that this spot of earth has laid claim to Naomi, its spiritual deed of ownership displayed on her serene face.

Evening walks are a solace, she says, best savored with her husband of more than twenty years, Larry Strickland, whom

Naomi began dating during her early days in Nashville. A former bass singer for Elvis Presley and member of the famed J. D. Sumner and the Stamps Quartet, Larry currently performs with the Palmetto State Quartet, a southern gospel group.

Naomi beams as she points to the nearby creek and explains her enthrallment with a groundhog and armadillo that lived across the road last year. "I live in a *National Geographic* preservation," she says. "That entertains me."

Naomi's rags-to-riches epic is now legendary, a modern-day Jack tale straight out of Appalachian folklore. Few care that it has occasionally been colored and compressed and sanitized over the years, shaped by clever marketing executives and even by Naomi herself. What makes it resonate still, some twenty years after the Judds first disbanded, is that, as in all Jack tales, the scrappy hillbilly that everyone discounted was ultimately victorious. Naomi explains: "They called me 'everywoman.' I was the Cinderella story of country music."

At the age of thirty-seven, Naomi felt like the princess at the ball when the Judds' first single, "Had a Dream (for the Heart)," was released. Over the next eight years of their reign, Naomi and Wynonna watched single after single go to number one on the country charts: "Mama He's Crazy," "Why Not Me," "Girls Night Out," "Love Is Alive," "Have Mercy," "Grandpa (Tell Me 'bout the Good Old Days)," "Rockin' with the Rhythm of the Rain," "Cry Myself to Sleep," "I Know Where I'm Going," "Maybe Your Baby's Got the Blues," "Turn It Loose," "Change of Heart," "Young Love (Strong Love)," and "Let Me Tell You about Love."

She dressed the part, too, hiring an audacious designer named Esben to create her colorful costumes. "What would the average woman wear if she got to play Carnegie Hall or Madison Square Garden?" Naomi asked herself one evening at her house on Del Rio Pike. "Wouldn't you just say, 'I'm gonna wear the most outrageous Technicolor outfit I can wear, and I'm gonna jump off risers and have spike heels and flirt with the band and accept roses from the guys in the front row?' I thought it was far more interesting going onstage singing 'Kentucky, you are the dearest land outside of heaven to me' looking like that, with five layers of colorful petticoats and huge colored glass jewelry that sparkled to the back row."

Naomi and Wynonna's modern style was a contrast to their acoustic sound. The Judds presaged a return to traditional country music in the 1980s, plowing the ground for roots-based performers such as Keith Whitley, Kathy Mattea, and Randy Travis. "I remember there was a thing in *Time* magazine that said, 'The Judds save country music,' because it was after *Urban Cowboy* and Barbara Mandrell and Kenny Rogers," Naomi notes.

The Country Music Association apparently agreed, expressing its appreciation by naming the duo Vocal Group of the Year for an unprecedented seven consecutive years. But perhaps even more important was the Grammy Awards' support of traditional country music, demonstrated by the Judds' five trophies, followed by another for Naomi as cowriter of 1992's Best Country Song, "Love Can Build a Bridge." Despite such accolades, Naomi says she never forgot her heritage, declaring herself "a front porch Kentucky girl."

Many Appalachians tend to be suspicious when one of their own has any measure of success, so it's only natural for me to wonder aloud if Naomi was ever accused of "getting above her raising" by folks back home in Ashland. She considers this for a moment as she takes a drink of water. "If anything, it was the other way around," she admits. "I was often too corny—I was guilty. I tried too hard because we'd found a niche and reveled in it."

"There's a tape of Wynonna and I on the *Ralph Emery Show*. I was wearing my apron, I had my hair jacked to Jesus, and I was making lye soap. I mean, Loretta Lynn looks like she's street smart or something. And frankly, I'd go home and my family was like, 'Have you ever seen Dolly naked?'" She cackles and slaps the arm of her chair. "You know, they wanted to know all that stuff!"

After the laughter subsides, Naomi grows wistful as she reminisces about being onstage with Wynonna. "We would be surrounded by blackness, and Wynonna and I would be singing to each other. Her voice is so luscious. We'd hit these tones, and if I did my part, we'd just feel it coming out of our fingertips. We just were absolutely zapped." She stops, allowing this image to sink in. "And you know that's why I'm a medical miracle—the Farewell Tour."

Looking at her today, her hazel eyes brimming with verve, it's easy to forget that Naomi was handed a virtual death sentence when she was diagnosed with hepatitis C in early 1990. She had been neglecting her health for a while, rationalizing that her fans and employees were counting on her to perform. Feeling fatigued, she finally had a blood test that led to the dire diagnosis. After countless doctor visits and treatments and much soul-searching, she announced her retirement later that year at an emotional press conference in the old RCA building, in the same room where she and Wynonna had auditioned seven years earlier. But remarkably, instead of going home to bed, Naomi insisted on embarking on a yearlong Farewell Tour that would take the Judds to 120 cities across the country. The concerts became an extension of her growing belief in alternative medicine and the power of the mind and spirit over the body. Culminating in a final concert on 4 December 1991 in Murfreesboro, Tennessee, the Farewell Tour became Naomi Judd's healer.

"It elevated my immune system," she explains in full nurse mode. "Music is mind. You have those stage lights—this warmth—and you feel like [a] chakra is opening up. When you have all those things together, you not only feel it, but because we're electrobio-magnetic energy fields, it goes out to the audience."

Today, Naomi has no symptoms of the disease and is in total remission. Her retirement has become null, filled with many professional responsibilities and achievements. She became the first national spokesperson for the American Liver Foundation and remains in demand as a motivational speaker and lecturer.

Her autobiography, *Love Can Build a Bridge,* spent ten weeks on the *New York Times* best-seller list and was made into a television movie. Other best-selling titles have followed: *Naomi's Home Companion, Naomi's Breakthrough Guide, The Transparent Life,* and *Naomi's Guide to Aging Gratefully,* as well as three children's books.

Branching out into television, she starred in three television movies—*Rio Diablo, A Song for the Season,* and *The Killing Game*—hosted a talk show, *Naomi's New Morning,* on the Hallmark Channel for two seasons, and served as a judge and mentor on *Can You Duet,* a country music reality series conceived by the producers of *American Idol.*

In 2000 she reunited with Wynonna for the Power to Change Tour, performing in thirty cities before more than 300,000 fans. But even that did not mark the end of the Judds. After periodically reteaming for special events over the years, the duo announced in 2010 that they were embarking on a final concert tour billed as the Last Encore. When the string of buses rolled into Louisville for the tour's sole Kentucky date at the brand-new KFC Yum! Center, the atmosphere had the feel of a family reunion. "We're home!" Naomi exclaimed from the stage, prompting a roar from the capacity crowd that included a healthy mix of young and elderly couples, middle-aged women with their daughters, and gay men in droves.

Backstage, Naomi and Wynonna were tailed by a camera crew filming a docuseries based on their musical reunion and the emotional journey of their complex relationship, produced by the newly created Oprah Winfrey Network (OWN). *The Judds* debuted in April 2011 as one of OWN's first original productions, an "irresistibly broken-hearted" portrait of a relationship "very much like mothers and daughters of a certain age and demographic," according to the *Washington Post*.

Despite all her years in the spotlight, what gives Naomi the most pride, she says, is her family. As a solo artist, Wynonna has sold more than ten million albums and was hailed by *Rolling Stone* as "the greatest female country singer since Patsy Cline." Much of her time is spent raising her two children, Elijah and Grace, on a farm that adjoins Naomi's.

Ashley is a Golden Globe–nominated actress who in recent years has become a passionate activist, serving as Global Ambassador for YouthAIDS, fighting mountaintop removal mining in Appalachia, earning a master's degree from Harvard University's John F. Kennedy School of Government, and penning a *New York Times* best-selling memoir titled *All That Is Bitter and Sweet*. She divides her time between Leipers Fork and Scotland, where she lives with her husband, car racer Dario Franchitti, two-time winner of the Indianapolis 500.

"It thrills my entire being to read an article where Ashley starts out saying, 'I'm a proud eighth-generation Kentuckian,'" Naomi says. "I like to know that they're carrying on a tradition. I don't think we have enough spokespeople in Kentucky. There aren't enough political figures; there aren't enough honorable celebrities. On a deeply personal level, I feel better that the girls remember Aunt Pauline."

Her most enduring legacy, then, might also be the most implausible: that her daughters, uprooted so many times during childhood, have retained an astoundingly stalwart sense of place. "It's all ancestral memory," she says. "It still courses through our veins."

In the throes of her bout with hepatitis, a crass reporter asked Naomi at a press conference what she planned to use as her epitaph. Momentarily taken aback, she quickly regained her composure and fashioned a remarkably articulate response. "I said, 'I want to be known as a godly woman who's from Kentucky.' That's it. Kentucky is past, present, and future for me."

Essential Tracks

"River of Time"
"Guardian Angels"
"Why Not Me"
"Change of Heart"
"Grandpa (Tell Me 'bout the Good Old Days)"

2

Ben Sollee and
Daniel Martin Moore

Sword and Snow

A lone note bowed from a weathered cello fills the performance
space of Louisville Public Media on Fourth Street in downtown
Louisville. Long and low, it blends with the animated conversations of the stream of people trickling into the room: hipsters in
skinny jeans and oversized beanies, businessmen and -women in
standard navy blue suits. They quickly fill up the seventy seats in
the small studio, and soon another sound is added to the impro-
vised orchestra—the rustling of brown paper bags being opened
as sandwiches and potato chips are consumed.

This is the meal portion of WFPK Radio Louisville's *Live
Lunch,* a Friday afternoon institution that has featured roots artists such as John Hiatt, the Carolina Chocolate Drops, and the
Drive-By Truckers, along with a variety of local and regional musicians, over the years. Today on the makeshift stage, Ben Sollee
and Daniel Martin Moore are intent on tuning their instruments.
Ben leans his head over the cello, his eyes obscured by locks of
sandy hair. Daniel nods to someone in the audience as he adjusts
the high E string on his guitar.

After a brief introduction by deejay Laura Shine, Ben and
Daniel launch into "Something Somewhere Sometime," the opening track of their just released album *Dear Companion,* which ex-

plores the pair's physical and spiritual connections to their native Kentucky and their feelings about mountaintop removal mining, a radical form of strip mining that has destroyed more than 700,000 acres of land in Appalachia.

"So turn on your city / and I will turn on mine," they croon over a pulsating beat provided by Dan Dorff on drums and Cheyenne Marie Mize on electric guitar, before breaking into an all-out jam featuring Ben's gritty, electrified cello. Many in the audience are aware of their own links to mountaintop removal (MTR) and the cheap electricity it ensures, but others are hearing this buzzword for the first time and look at their neighbors quizzically. Following the set, they line up at the information table for Appalachian Voices—a regional nonprofit that campaigns against mountaintop removal—to learn more. They are invited to visit the organization's website and plug in their zip codes to determine whether their electricity is derived from a mountaintop removal site. "All of Louisville gets its power from MTR," a college student mutters to her friend, her backpack emblazoned with a bumper sticker that reads "Mountain Justice." "Mine comes from Kayford Mountain in West Virginia."

Similar conversations take place later that evening at the Brown Theatre just down the street, where Ben and Daniel perform a full-blown show to a raucous, sold-out audience. Backstage, they wrap each other in a tight bear hug before returning to the stage for an encore, a cover of fellow Kentuckian Jean Ritchie's sing-along "Jubilee." When they venture out to the lobby to sign CDs, a fan grabs Daniel by the arm. "Great show," he says. "How did you guys hook up?"

Daniel turns to Ben and grins before responding: "MySpace."

It would be an understatement to say that the cello and roots music are not synonymous. Yet in many ways, it is the ideal folk instrument, capable of expressing a wide array of emotions in tones so mellow and deep that they nearly rattle one's very soul. This realization was not lost on music critics or listeners when Ben burst onto the national music scene in 2008 with his acclaimed debut *Learning to Bend,* a record that was hailed as "inventive" and "refreshing" for its fusion of folk, soul, and classical genres and led National Public Radio to laud him as one of the "Top Ten Great Unknown Artists of 2007."

That accolade was "a shocker," Ben recalls over a cup of tea. "I couldn't figure out why they were talking about it. It felt like there was a big focus on how alternatively I was playing the cello, when I felt I wasn't doing anything alternative at all."

Ben Sollee, Fund-Raiser

In mid-January 2012 Ben Sollee took to the Internet to raise money for his upcoming studio album *Half-Made Man.* Using Pledge Music, a website that bills itself as a "hands-on, direct-to-fan music-making" tool, he set a goal of collecting enough pledges to fully fund the record within sixty days, while setting aside 10 percent of his proceeds to benefit Oxfam America. In return for the financial support, Ben offered his fans special incentives: a digital download of the record for a $10 pledge, a Skype songwriting mentoring session (complete with digital download and T-shirt) for $170, a house concert performance for $2,500, and a signed cello for $7,500.

"We will meet the goal," he wrote in a message to his fans, but even he was astounded by the swift response to his call. Within four days of the campaign's kickoff, the project had received 263 pledges and was 101 percent funded. "I'm feeling a lot of love and a lot of pride in the work we're doing in the world," Ben said, thanking his funders. "Please keep sharing and telling the story."

A listen to *Learning to Bend* says otherwise. Ben's emotive style of playing creates a distinct, readily identifiable sound, one that melds his extensive musical training with a willingness to experiment. "*Learning to Bend* was a great way to crack myself open in a lot of ways," he admits. "It was kind of like all the pieces and parts of me. It swung in all the characters of my music."

The jazz-inflected "It's Not Impossible" has him alternately plucking, strumming, and bowing the cello, accented by a dissonant horn solo. "Panning for Gold," a song as gentle as a prayer, plays like a classical movement, his soft plucking overlaid with a lush, orchestral gauze. A rousing cover of Sam Cooke's "A Change Is Gonna Come," featuring additional lyrics by Ben, relies on a repetition of soulful bows and hums across the strings.

His musical wanderings through the realms of folk, soul, jazz, and classical demonstrate the versatility of the cello. But perhaps even more noteworthy, Ben uses the instrument to add an Appalachian flair to his songs. "Hang your worries on my thin Kentucky frame," he invites on the gentle "Built for This" as his cello drones, mimicking the peaks and valleys of the Cumberlands. Banjo and cello meet on "Bury Me with My Car," a bluegrass-tinged jam that mourns America's addiction to the internal combustion engine. "I've always loved the landscape of Kentucky, but it wasn't an intentional thing," he explains. "It was just Kentucky—that's where I'm from."

As a child growing up in Lexington, Ben would spend weekends in southeastern Kentucky with his grandfather, an Appalachian fiddler who taught him traditional tunes such as "Back Up and Push" and "Run Mule, Run." At home, his father played a rhythm and blues guitar that Ben often picked up and slowly began to learn. But then, at age nine, he was introduced to the cello in public school in Lexington. "I was all about gags back then," he admits, "so I chose it because I could make fart noises."

Ben Sollee's musical wanderings demonstrate the versatility of the cello. Perhaps even more noteworthy, he uses the instrument to add an Appalachian flair to his songs. (Photo by Meagan Jordan)

He was hooked. A couple of years later, he was writing songs, and by his freshman year of high school, he had started a band called Bliss on Tap. By age fifteen, he was hard at work making an album in his parents' basement. Titled *Just Plain Ben*, it featured an experimental set of socially conscious songs against a backdrop of cello, drums, and paint cans. So taken was Ben with the cello that when it came time to go to college, he entered the music program at the University of Louisville to study the instrument. Despite his love of music, he gave himself an ultimatum when he graduated: "I said, I want to give myself two years and see what's happening, and if nothing's happening, I'm going to grad school."

He need not have worried. After finishing school, Ben became a regular on the *Woodsongs Old-Time Radio Hour,* based in Lexington, and he toured China and the United States with banjo chanteuse Abigail Washburn as part of the Sparrow Quartet, which also included fiddler Casey Driessen and multiple Grammy Award–winner Béla Fleck. After recording a quiet album called *Turn on the Moon,* Ben turned his attention to the songs that became *Learning to Bend.*

With politically colored songs like "A Few Honest Words" and Ben's reworking of "A Change Is Gonna Come," the record became part of the national zeitgeist when it was released in 2008 amid the forces of change unleashed by Barack Obama's bid for the presidency. "It rode this wave as if I was talking about the Obama campaign," Ben recalls, "as if 'A Change Is Gonna Come' was some type of *fuck you* to the Bush administration and some type of big push behind Obama. It wasn't about that—it was antiwar. I could not figure out why we were at war in Iraq." These themes resonated with war-weary Americans across the country, as Ben found out when he embarked on a lengthy tour that fall. Following that jaunt, Ben began another in late spring 2009, an eight-day circuit that he completed entirely on bicycle. Destination: Bonnaroo, in Manchester, Tennessee.

With his cello strapped to the back of his Xtracycle, Ben and a group of friends began the 330-mile trek by taking to the back roads of Kentucky, playing shows in small towns along the way before crossing into Tennessee, where he performed a raucous set at the music festival. Proceeds from the tour, dubbed "Pedaling Against Poverty," benefited Oxfam International.

Ben's bicycle tour provided him with a lot of insight about Kentucky and its people, he says, describing how his bicycle's lack of "fancy shocks" allowed him to actually feel the state of the roads, which varied by county and neighborhood. "That defines socioeconomic stuff. Usually it relates to the conditions of houses, and usually it relates to the condition of the people living in the houses."

He also became more aware of the physical geography of his native state. "It's the hardest riding I've done anywhere in the country," he laughs. "Definitely the hardest ride. You just get a real appreciation for how different the landscape is here than anywhere else in the country. We just rode down through so many river valleys and lake beds. It's just up and down, up and down. It was really hard."

The long, arduous journey allowed Ben some much-needed time to reflect on his family's Kentucky heritage and his own musical identity, issues raised with the release of *Learning to Bend*. He quickly found that they were closely linked. "As more exposure came to my music, I was being forced to reach back to my roots," he says. "It wasn't part of our family tradition to talk about our heritage. I didn't really know my roots growing up."

That search for his familial and musical lineage led him "more and more" to both Appalachian folk music and the urban rhythm and blues he had heard and loved as a child growing up in the 1980s. He pauses, lost in thought for a moment, before taking a bite out of a scone. "I ended up with this music that was basically a portrait of who I was and where I came from."

Daniel Martin Moore was visiting a friend's house when he noticed an ancient parlor-style classical guitar standing in the corner of the living room. He studied it intently and later found himself thinking about it during his classes at Northern Kentucky University and wondering, during gigs as a wedding photographer, if he could learn to play it. Finally, on a return trip, he summoned the courage to ask if he could borrow it. After receiving permission, he took it home, gave it a good cleaning, and had it restrung at a local guitar shop. Then he set out to learn to play it. "The action was probably an inch high and I couldn't hardly play it, but it was really beautiful," he laughs now, leaning against a sycamore on his family's land just outside Elizabethtown, Kentucky, on a muggy summer afternoon. "It was transformative."

Five years later, Daniel had signed a record deal with the independent powerhouse label Sub-Pop—the home of acclaimed artists Iron & Wine and Fleet Foxes—and released his debut album, *Stray Age,* an introspective collection of original songs, including the sprightly shuffle "That'll Be the Plan" and the haunting piano ballad "By Dream," along with a gorgeous reading of Fairport Convention's standard "Who Knows Where the Time Goes."

The record showcases Daniel's voice, an instrument as smooth as birch bark that was honed in a pew alongside his mother and grandmother at the First Christian Church in Elizabethtown. "I just absorbed all of those hymns," he smiles, ticking off a string of his favorites: "Softly and Tenderly," "Just a Closer Walk with Thee," "It Is Well with My Soul." "There's a simplicity to them that just sort of hits home with me."

Their influence can also be felt in his graceful songwriting, replete with soothing images of trees and birds and tea. "Come be close and be rested," Daniel beckons on the title track, and indeed, the entire album is as comforting and familiar as a cup of Earl Grey with milk, sugared with his unadorned guitar playing. It is no wonder that Daniel made history at Sub-Pop, becoming the first artist in the label's twenty-year history who was signed on the strength of his demo alone, a serendipitous tale in itself.

Daniel had just returned from a brief stint in the Peace Corps, serving in the western African nation of Cameroon before being stricken with a debilitating *E. coli* infection, followed by amoebas and then a cold. ("I got a cold in the jungle of all places!" he mourns with a mock laugh.) He moved in with his older brother in Minneapolis to recuperate and began recording some original songs in his brother's studio to pass the time. When he finished, he sent them "on a whim" to a few independent record labels, including Sub-Pop, in January 2007. Four months later, he was house-sitting in Costa Rica for a friend he had made in the Peace Corps when he received an e-mail from Sub-Pop requesting more material. "So I just made a bunch of recordings there in Costa

Ol Kentuck Recordings

With the national hunger for roots music, the availability of recording technology, and the democratization of the Internet, independent music is thriving. Musicians can now record quality albums in their homes, drop off the finished products at their local record stores, and post the albums on iTunes. Small, indie record labels are flourishing, and Ol Kentuck Recordings is no exception. Launched by Daniel Martin Moore in the spring of 2011, the label already boasts a handful of roots artists, including former Over the Rhine guitarist Ric Hordinski, the all-female traditional trio Maiden Radio, banjo player Joan Shelley, and multi-instrumentalist Daniel Joseph Dorff.

"My hope is to continue to use Ol Kentuck to help release great projects by artists that might not otherwise happen," Daniel says of the label, "and also to use it to do a few things I've been meaning to do for a while—collaborative projects, mostly. . . . That's basically the heart of the label."

Rica and e-mailed them," he says. "It just sort of all worked out." Daniel signed the recording contract on his twenty-fifth birthday, returning the document to the label via an international phone fax that cost eight dollars.

When *Stray Age* was released later that year, he laid aside plans to attend graduate school, deciding to concentrate on his music as a career, not simply a pastime, which he describes as "the most exciting part" of his record deal. Given that his only live performances consisted of playing at a local coffeehouse on a few occasions, Daniel was not eager to tour. "Sometimes it's pretty ugly for the first song or two," he laughs about his anxiety, "but once it settles down, it's a joy."

Daniel makes no apologies for being rooted in Kentucky or for choosing to continue to be based there, even if it is sometimes inconvenient for his career. "It's not important enough to me to make it as a musician if I have to leave my home to do it," he says. "I'd rather do something else and have music as a big part of my life but my life *here*."

A bead of sweat trickles down his brow, and he pauses to capture it before turning a bottle of ice-cold water up to his mouth. A comfortable silence descends, punctuated only by the occasional birdcall. He breaks the silence by pointing out a thicket of trees he used to play in with his brother and sister. "Growing up here has connected me to my family and to the land," he offers, before describing his family's move to the northern Kentucky suburb of Cold Spring when he was eight years old, following his parents' divorce. There, he cultivated his ties to the land by playing in the small patch of woods behind his new house and eventually discovered the music of fellow Kentuckian Jean Ritchie. "There's no comparison," he says of Ritchie. "She's my favorite for so many reasons."

Daniel takes a slice of Kentucky on the road with him by playing a traditional ballad at each stop, both as a tribute to Ritchie and as a means of combating his bouts of chronic homesickness. "A lot of people have never heard them," he says of the ballads, shaking his head. "I try to pick one that's kind of accessible and somewhat short, because most of them are a little overwhelming. An eleven-minute version of 'Lord Randall'—most people can't handle that."

The influence of Appalachian music and how it has been passed down through successive generations of musicians is a subject that captivates Daniel, and he muses about it at length. "I came to those folk songs not directly," he explains of his own introduction to them. "I don't remember my grandmother singing 'Barbry Allen' or anything like that. But as I learned them—as I heard Jean Ritchie singing them, and Bascam Lamar Lunsford and people like that—I instantly recognized how those songs informed all the songs that I really loved." Those acts of preservation, he says, continue to inspire his own songwriting. "Music for me is a respite. If the music I make can be that for someone else, then that would be one way to measure the success of it."

Picture it: Sixth and Main Streets in Louisville on 12 June 1931. After a flurry of telegrams and letters, legendary producer and talent scout Ralph Peer has persuaded two of the country's most popular musical acts to record together in an empty storefront turned RCA Victor mobile recording studio. In the work space are a trio of musicians known as the Carter Family and a tall, slender man in the throes of tuberculosis named Jimmie Rodgers. Over the course of a long day, the musicians record fictitious "visits" to their respective homes in Maces Springs, Virginia, and Kerrville, Texas.

Cut to nearly eighty years later: downtown Lexington just off Winchester Road. Ben and Daniel are in the studio at Shangri-la Productions recording *Dear Companion,* their musical partnership forged by the modern marvel known as social networking. Instead of sending a telegram from his home in Lexington north to Cold Spring, Ben logged on to his MySpace account and typed a message to Daniel after hearing his song "Flyrock Blues," about mountaintop removal mining.

Ben had recently learned about the destructive effects of mountaintop removal in his native state and was interested in addressing the issue in his music. "I started looking for somebody to share it with," he explains. "I didn't want it to be like one man's protest. I really wanted it to be a shared front. It's more than just one person's thing. So I found Daniel's music online and sent him a message."

Daniel had learned about the disastrous form of strip mining in high school, and his awareness of it heightened when he read Kentucky author Erik Reece's *Lost Mountain* and got involved with Kentuckians for the Commonwealth, a grassroots organization that seeks to end the practice. He says that Ben's e-mail caught him by surprise. "I had not heard his music before, but I listened to it as soon as I got his e-mail. I was really impressed. It was beautiful stuff."

More messages followed, and Ben finally ventured out to one of Daniel's live shows. "We ended up meeting," Daniel continues. "We had coffee and just talked about music. And we just kept talking about doing some songs and making some recordings about trying to raise awareness about mountaintop removal." Ben convinced Daniel to partner on an EP, and together they recruited My Morning Jacket front man and fellow Kentuckian Jim James to come aboard as producer.

But the two new friends swiftly realized that the project required a full-length album, an opus that fused the influences of Kentucky's natural world with its storied musical heritage. "We ex-

Ben Sollee and Daniel Martin Moore, backed by Daniel Joseph Dorff, at a concert in Louisville. (Photo by Matthew McCardwell)

plicitly wanted to bring in Appalachia and just the sound of it, the feel of it, the stories from it," says Ben, "but we didn't want it to be an homage to some old recording." With this in mind, the two crafted an album that is modern Kentucky roots music at its finest, a cutting-edge record with subtle nods to a more traditional era.

At first glance, theirs appeared to be an odd pairing: Ben, a classically trained musician and gritty singer steeped in blue-eyed soul, and Daniel, a self-taught guitarist and confessed folkie with a velveteen croon. Yet in the studio, their voices crystallized, producing rich, tight harmonies reminiscent of the Everly Brothers, another pair of Kentuckians who helped reshape roots music.

"I had convention to throw away, and he had convention to learn," Ben laughs. "And we kind of met on a table right in the middle there somewhere." Both agreed on an important point, he says: "[The record] didn't need to be *look at these people's lives and how hard they have it.* It needed to be *look how we're all involved in these people's lives.*"

Each brought a series of original songs to the table, and they collaborated on two: a soaring elegy called "Sweet Marie" and the title track, which they envisioned as a "letter from Appalachia to the rest of the nation," says Daniel. The song "Dear Companion," its title a nod to a beloved Jean Ritchie composition, was inspired by a message penned by a dying miner to his wife while he was trapped underground (reprinted in Appalachian historian Ronald Eller's landmark book *Uneven Ground*). The note further humanized the issue of coal mining for Ben and Daniel, who wanted to present the complexities of both living in Appalachia and residing in cities tied to the region through electricity, or "putting a human face to the power," Ben explains.

The driving instrumentation of the opening track, "Something Somewhere Sometime," recalls the dozers and draglines hauling out the coal, underscored by Ben's deep cello and a circular banjo hook provided by Jim. The song offers an apology to both the land and the people of Appalachia: "If I've wounded you, I'm sorry / I had good intentions."

"People that grew up in the cities are tied to Appalachia," says Ben. "[The song] is very much about the Industrial Revolution and all the stuff that set into motion, [all the things] that we expect in our lives but are also powered by the tremendously old—really devastating—technology."

Despite the underlying message of their music, both Ben and Daniel took great care to ensure that the record did not turn into a polemic. "We didn't necessarily want it to be a protest record," Ben explains. "We wanted it to be a record that was supported by Appalachia and talked about the issues there, but in the bigger light." Daniel concurs: "We're not experts and scholars. We don't want to go out and preach to people. We just want to point [them] in the right direction." That route was Appalachian Voices, to which Ben and Daniel donated 100 percent of their artist royalties.

When it was released in February 2010, *Dear Companion* was hailed by *Paste Magazine* as a "far from preachy" portrait of these issues "through an unmistakably human lens." This review struck particularly close to home for Ben. Two days after the record was released, he discovered that his own family's land had been strip-mined with the permission of his grandparents. "I made a record to find that out," he marvels, shaking his head. "It was like this rollback in time to a decision that economically made it possible for a family to step up to a new level. There's no way that my mom would have been in the economic position to go to college. She wouldn't have met my dad, she wouldn't have had me; they wouldn't have been in a position to put me in music. That rehumanized things for me even more [in] this coal debate."

Such personal connections to the issue added yet another layer of passion to their music. After an initial round of tour dates that kicked off with their show in Louisville, Ben and Daniel hit the road again that summer, this time with Jim James in tow, on a series of nine concerts throughout Appalachia that culminated at the Newport Folk Festival. Billed as the Appalachian Voices Tour, a portion of the proceeds once again benefited Appalachian Voices.

In a world of deafening cross talk on cable news shows and strident op-eds, Ben and Daniel felt that using their art was the best way to raise the issue of mountaintop removal. "We wanted to make a record that we really hope people will like and be interested in," Daniel says, "even if they know nothing about mountaintop removal, and we can use it to draw them in. Even if it's just that fleeting moment where it just enters their consciousness, you never know how that's going to affect things down the road if it comes up on a ballot or they hear a politician talking about it. You never know what that's going to do."

A year later, Ben takes the stage of the Kentucky Theatre in downtown Lexington to whoops and hollers from a packed house. He raises the cello in his right hand in a gesture of acknowledgment, provoking even greater applause. Ever the gentleman, he bows before taking his seat center stage. Seconds later, a military-style drumbeat kicks in, joined by a bass guitar and Ben's evocative cello. This interlude then gives way to his distinctive voice, a weathered instrument that sounds much older than his twenty-seven years, filling every nook and cranny of the hall: "Sometimes, I wear feathers to feel close to the sky / When I turn out the lights I am part of the night."

By the time he reaches the chorus, a dissonant horn section has joined in, creating an ethereal countermelody that causes many in the audience to lean forward in their red-cushioned seats. This song, "Close to You," is new to them, and they want to catch every lyric and horn trill. They are a hometown crowd, gathered to support their native son as he marks the release of his third album, *Inclusions.* A departure of sorts from *Learning to Bend* and *Dear Companion,* the record challenges conventional definitions of folk music, exploring the boundaries—or the lack thereof—of the genre.

"We seem to confuse the *tradition* of folk music with folk music," he says of the new record. "We are living in more cities than ever, and those cities are denser than they've ever been. So what does that mean to our idea of folk music? What does it mean when people are living next door to each other and one person has their family recordings of their grandmother singing Balkan folk music [and their neighbor] is listening to really hard-core, homemade hip-hop? What does *that* sound like?"

Inclusions is the direct product of Ben's journey to unearth his cultural and musical roots, a fusion of the Appalachian folk music of his grandfather and the urban rhythm and blues he was exposed to as a child in Lexington. This musical melting pot provided the record with its title. But Ben is quick to explain that it also refers to his concept of the arts, communities, and personal relationships. "I love this record," he confesses. "I love it for all of its meanings, explicit and incidental. In these songs, I can hear the city I grew up in and the people that lived down the street."

Ben condenses these influences in songs like "Embrace," where the slight dip of the bow on his cello and in his voice recalls a mountain ballad from Appalachia. Or Kazakhstan. These styles, he points out, are remarkably similar and express the universality of the record itself: "People hear themselves in it."

"Bible Belt" is a standout track that further illustrates this point, with its pointed lyrics describing how the outside world often invades a couple's intimacy with its social mores and prejudices, preventing inclusion and acceptance. "We didn't ask your permission / And I won't wear your bible belt," he declares, his voice rife with defiance over the contrasting reverberations of gentle drum brushes and jarring horns.

In a society that demands neat, constrictive labels, Ben is all over the map. He recalls an animated discussion with his manager and publicist over how to categorize the album. They balked when he insisted on labeling it folk. "They're like, 'People don't think of folk music like you think of folk music.'" He explains his stance this way: "That's the point of the conversation—this is *contemporary* folk."

Just as he transcends boundaries between musical genres, Ben is also hoping to bridge the divides between artistic vocations, fusing music with film and dance and performance art. This, he believes, is a large step toward community development. "I'm hoping to be able to use music and the arts to get rural communities performing, to help them grow and be a part of the national conversation in a bigger way." The key, he argues, is cultural pride. "The reason New York has so much influence from a media standpoint is it has that empowerment thing—*we are New York*. So I [feel] like taking that approach with Kentucky: *We are Kentucky. We are Louisville. We are Lexington. We are hugely influenced by Appalachia*."

Onstage in Lexington, Ben strums his mellow electric guitar, eyes closed, head bobbing along with the light sift of the brushes across the snare drum. Many in the crowd follow suit. Others remain motionless, allowing the lush tones to sink in. Like the music, the audience is diverse, a blending of ages, ethnicities, and backgrounds, defying categorization. Distilled to one word, it too would have to be described as *folk*.

Ben glances up and smiles ever so slightly, knowing that *Inclusions* is not just an album title—it is a community meant to be savored.

"I'm being dominated by this track right now," Daniel complains good-naturedly, throwing down his headphones in a small studio at WXVU Radio in Cincinnati. He and a group of musicians, including multi-instrumentalist Dan Dorff, are laying down tracks for his second solo album, *In the Cool of the Day,* a collection of traditional hymns and four original compositions.

The guitar player is running late, but Daniel is unfazed, moving to the control booth to whip up a mixture of his vocal tonic of hot water, ginger root, and honey to dispense among the singers. After it cools, he takes a sip and allows an extended sigh to escape his lungs. "Just try it both ways," Daniel calls to Dorff, who is still rehearsing. "Don't overthink it."

The errant guitarist eventually arrives, and after several more takes, the band is in the zone, reinventing the old standard "Up

"What's wonderful about so many of the old hymns is their austerity, depth, and poetry. It's what gives them their staying power." —Daniel Martin Moore (Photo by Matthew McCardwell)

above My Head" with a swinging guitar and a jazzy beat. When it comes time to record his vocal, Daniel alters only one word of the original lyrics—changing "God" to "joy"—a variation that captures the song's mood perfectly.

The change could serve as a metaphor for the album itself, for what gives *In the Cool of the Day* its transcendent quality is Daniel's decision to weave his own theology into some of the older songs while remaining true to their spirit. Such a choice might have proved disastrous, but he is a master of subtlety, with these seemingly small details extending an invitation to the nonreligious to move beyond the old-fashioned dogma of gospel music and simply appreciate its art.

"Much of the mystery, joy, and simplicity of a thoughtful life is lost in the legalism and the rigidity of the answers that seem to have been created to support the brick-and-mortar side of religion," he says later. *In the Cool of the Day* razes that restrictive building one track at a time, celebrating the sheer poetry of hymnody and challenging what he sees as the superficiality of modern praise music. "It's the contrived pop-ness of it that doesn't appeal to me," he explains. "It's also how generic the lyrics usually are that gets at me. What's wonderful about so many of the old hymns is their austerity, depth, and poetry. It's what gives them their staying power. Most of the new praise music feels like a cheap, dressed-up copy of a pop song by comparison." Daniel offers up the title track, an environmental psalm penned by his musical heroine Jean Ritchie, as an anecdote. "This earth is a garden, the garden of my Lord," he sings lightly, almost to himself.

Gospel is a genre that is notorious for vocalists who over-sing, belting out the lyrics in a feeble attempt to imitate artists such as Mavis Staples. But not Daniel. His vocals are crisp and understated, as on the classic hymn "Softly and Tenderly," which features an achingly beautiful cello, courtesy of Ben, and sterling harmony vocals from alt-country singer-songwriter Haley Bonar.

When it was released in January 2011, *In the Cool of the Day* was dubbed "uniformly gorgeous" by *Pitchfork,* with Daniel's original compositions attracting special attention. The new material melds seamlessly with the traditional hymns, from the soothing one-minute opener, "All Ye Tenderhearted," to the album's centerpiece, "O My Soul," a gentle march in which he proclaims, "Each step a living prayer / And we never walk alone," over his own gorgeous piano. The contemplative "Set Things Aright," the album's final track, provides an elegant coda, with Daniel's tender vocals blending with those of Jim James and Bonar.

"I'm calling it a folk-gospel-country-jazz album," he chuckles, before getting serious and returning to the subject of cultural and musical preservation. "Those are the songs I grew up hearing all the time, that I loved as a child and love now. It just [seemed] like the right thing to do."

Ben and Daniel stand in the foreground of a sweeping arc of purple lights onstage at the Louisville Palace Theatre. They are the special musical guests of Jim James and My Morning Jacket, who have staged a hometown concert to launch the group's latest album, *Circuital*. It is an event being filmed by Academy Award–nominated director Todd Haynes (*I'm Not There, Far from Heaven*) and streamed live on YouTube.

"Those guys are so different," Jim declared with a broad grin during an interview a few weeks earlier. "I always said that Ben reminded me of a sword and Daniel reminded me of soft, falling snow, and together they made this really cool image in my head. It was a thrill for me to see these two completely different forces that are Kentucky, and see them push for something so positive."

As Jim approaches the mike, Ben takes a seat, his legs hugging his ever-present cello. Daniel approaches him quietly, and they exchange a break-a-leg fist bump before Jim launches into "Wonderful (The Way I Feel)." By the time the second verse rolls around, the generous Jim cedes the spotlight to the boys. Daniel closes his eyes and cups his hand, crooning the lyrics to a burst of loud applause over Ben's lush cello. When Jim claims the lead once again on the chorus, Daniel transitions to a rich harmony.

"Mr. Daniel Martin Moore and Mr. Ben Sollee," Jim announces to the crowd as the last chord fades. "God bless 'em."

Essential Tracks

Ben Sollee and Daniel Martin Moore

"My Wealth Comes to Me"
"Dear Companion"
"Something Somewhere Sometime"
"Needn't Say a Thing"

Ben Sollee

"Built for This"
"It's Not Impossible"
"Only a Song"
"Bible Belt"
"Electrified"

Daniel Martin Moore

"That'll Be the Plan"
"By Dream"
"Dark Road"
"O My Soul"
"The Cool of the Day"

3

Chris Knight

Trailer Poet

It was supposed to be the year of the rural film. Going into the Seventy-eighth Academy Awards ceremony, held at the Kodak Theatre in Hollywood in early March 2006, odds were on the groundbreaking drama *Brokeback Mountain,* the story of two cowboys falling in love in the wilds of Wyoming, winning the Oscar for Best Motion Picture. It was a done deal—or so everyone thought—when Jack Nicholson sauntered across the stage to present the award. After introducing the nominees, he opened the envelope and allowed a tinge of surprise to cloud his iconic voice: "And the Oscar goes to . . . *Crash!*" Some in the audience audibly gasped. Raising his eyebrows, Nicholson mouthed "Whoa!" to someone offstage.

Backstage, *Brokeback Mountain* co-screenwriter Larry McMurtry, legendary author of the rural novels *Lonesome Dove* and *The Last Picture Show,* was not shocked in the least. "Members of the Academy are not rural people," he explained to the Associated Press. "We are an urban nation. We are not a rural nation. It's not easy even to get a rural story made."

This was not news to people from Kentucky, a largely rural state made up of small towns like Slaughters, population 238. Tucked away in the northwestern part of the state, it's a community that many in the big-city media might dismiss as a cultural backwater. Slaughters has no grand buildings on its Main Street and no large businesses, for that matter—only houses with giant oak trees sprouting from neat front yards, coal mines, and the CSX Railroad that slices through the hamlet. But what this town does have are stories—tons of them, in fact, just waiting to be told. Even the founding of Slaughters has taken on legendary status among the townspeople: local tradition has it that the town was named for one Gustavus G. Slaughter, who won the right to name the hamlet and the post office by winning a card game in 1855.

For years, alternative country singer-songwriter and Slaughters native Chris Knight has been a keeper of these stories, many of which have shown up in his music—seven albums of songs set mostly in and around his hometown. Many of his characters are what people in this part of the country would call "pure outlaws": there's the wild cardplayer and shooter in "Becky's Bible," the rowdy teenage boys of "Oil Patch Town," and the meth cookers of "Hell Ain't Half Full." And every now and then, he allows his more tranquil side to shine through, writing about the young "river rat" of "The River's Own" and the reformed sinner traveling "The Lord's Highway." All portray rural people as complex individuals, neither romanticized nor vilified.

"I just wrote what I knew," he says modestly, quietly, in an accent that is perpetually tied to the region's rolling hills and rich earth. "I just did it the way I saw it."

Country people are known to be stubborn. It's a philosophy that has generally served them well, carrying them through farm foreclosures, droughts, and coal mining disasters. But these days, their tenacity seems to be focused on maintaining their physical geography and personal dignity, both of which are necessary for remaining rural in an urban world.

Chris is country to the bone, one of those quiet men whose determination is lodged in the steeliness of his voice and carriage. His beefy frame makes it clear that he has known hard work. Even now, on one of the hottest days of the summer, he is building a barn on his forty-acre piece of property. His biceps bulge from the rolled sleeves of his trademark T-shirt: you know he could whip your ass if he took a notion to. But his strength isn't confined to his physical presence—it's a case of body mimicking soul. And this, he believes, comes from the land itself, the rolling landscape that he has steadfastly refused to leave.

"It's beautiful out here," he says with more than a shred of defiance. "I wouldn't want to live anywhere else. I live out in the hills. I don't even like to go to town."

When Chris was signed to a deal with Decca Records, a major country music label, in 1998, he was beside himself with excitement. But instead of making the conventional move—using

Chris Knight's Songwriting Roots

After picking up the guitar in his teens, Chris did what many young adults do when their attention turns elsewhere—he sold it.

"I didn't have a guitar for a couple of years," he remembers. That changed in 1986 with the release of Steve Earle's debut, *Guitar Town*. Songs like "Hillbilly Highway" and "Someday" renewed Chris's creativity, and he knew what he had to do: "I stopped at a guitar shop and bought a hundred-dollar guitar."

With his new instrument in tow, Chris began playing live—mostly covers, but soon an original song made it onto his set list. "I started writing some songs that stuck around for a while, and I'd play them for people, and they seemed to like them, even though they weren't finished songs. I bet I wrote sixty to seventy songs after I wrote the first that I thought was any good."

his advance as a down payment on a home in Nashville, for instance—he bought a house trailer and set it on a forty-acre piece of land just outside of Slaughters that he had purchased while working for the Kentucky Department of Surface Mining Reclamation and Enforcement. For Chris, this wasn't a change of pace: Before signing his record contract, he would drive back and forth to Nashville to pitch songs he had written and shop around his demo tape. Now, he made the trek to record his album and play gigs, opening for country music mainstays like Emmylou Harris and Alison Krauss.

"I think people were disappointed that I bought a new trailer," he sighs. "I lived in it for eleven years, wrote all those songs in it. They were afraid I wasn't going to be able to write anymore."

In spite of his record company's fears, Chris's lifestyle provided a natural marketing angle when his eponymous album was released in early 1998: Decca Records signs authentic country artist. The press latched on to his refusal to leave Slaughters, realizing that it made compelling copy. Nearly every article and review focused on the fact that Chris lived in a trailer. Most journalists approached the subject with dignity, but some were condescending, a fact that causes him to wonder aloud about an inherent misunderstanding of rural culture among the national, mostly urban-based media. "They think, 'Well, there aren't that many people that live in house trailers writing songs for six years before they ever go to Nashville,'" he scoffs, knowing full well that just the opposite is true.

In spite of the big city–small town tension, the press appreciated Chris's ability to tell a good tale. "An impressive set of original story-songs," wrote *Entertainment Weekly* in a glowing review of *Chris Knight*. "Often cinematic in his imagery and spare on instrumentation, he's best at profiling dark characters whose violence bubbles just below the surface."

Chris Knight. (Photo by Mark Tucker)

The album showcases the complexities of rural life, portraying its people as three-dimensional characters instead of mere superficial stereotypes. In "Love and a .45," a cop and a prostitute find love despite being on opposite sides of the law. "William," a somber tune about a boy who "grew up hard and mean" at the hands of an abusive father, describes how he repeats the cycle as an adult with his own family and community.

"I find rural characters to be a lot more interesting," Chris explains. "If I'm going to watch a movie, I don't necessarily want to see a science fiction movie or something about getting lost or anything like that. I like to watch stuff in rural settings with rural people."

Despite—or more likely because of—the record's literary quality, it failed to make an impact on the mainstream country charts of the late 1990s, which were dominated by the likes of Shania Twain, Faith Hill, and Kenny Chesney. Decca dropped Chris, and that might have been the end of the story. But these were also the early years of the alt-country movement, and *Chris Knight* had been noticed by many in Nashville who yearned for a return to a more traditional and authentic sound. Less than three years later, he had signed another recording contract, this time with Dualtone Records, an independent label specializing in Americana artists. He was ready to give it another shot.

"I'm glad to be here with these guys today," Chris smiles from the stage of the Ford Theater at the Country Music Hall of Fame in Nashville. "I'm glad to see you all." As part of an event dubbed "Picks and Pens," the brainchild of dynamo artist manager and fellow Kentuckian Kathi Whitley, he is here to talk about the cross-pollination of music and literature alongside fellow singer-songwriter Scott Miller and best-selling southern novelists William Gay and Silas House. Part concert, part reading and discussion, the show has attracted a healthy audience on a sunny Saturday afternoon in November.

"Scott was talking about sharing ideas, reading a book and the writer sharing that idea with you," Chris says. "John Steinbeck shared an idea with me quite a few years ago. I was supposed to read a book by Steinbeck called *The Grapes of Wrath* when I was in college, and I think I finally got around to reading it about ten years later. And as soon as I read it, I wanted to write this song to basically just paraphrase the book. This song's called 'Broken Plow.'"

Pausing for a split second, Chris begins picking out a stark, rolling rhythm on his guitar. The brooding tones of the minor key pull the audience headlong into the song's narrative even before he starts to sing: "Load up the old Dodge truck / We'll leave what we can't sell." By the time he reaches the end, when the family of sharecroppers has realized that "The Promised Land / Ain't as promising as it seems," the crowd rewards him with a crash of applause. He looks down and studies his guitar, shifting in his seat. After all these years in the business, he still hasn't made peace with being onstage, even though his place as a seminal roots artist is more than assured.

But this level of success wasn't clear in 2001, when Chris was one of the first artists to sign with the burgeoning roots label Dualtone. For his first indie outing, he was paired with former Georgia Satellite Dan Baird, who stepped into the role of producer. Together, the duo created *A Pretty Good Guy,* a record whose gritty sound matches the raucous characters of Chris's songs. The magazine *No Depression* praised the latter as "a collection of short stories and character sketches, drawn in details so sharp they can hurt."

Chris and Baird reteamed two years later for *The Jealous Kind,* adding Joe Hardy as coproducer. The Dust Bowl ballad "Broken Plow" set the tone for the record, another hardscrabble collection of songs in which the main characters rob a gas station, total cars, and commit domestic violence. But *The Jealous Kind* was also remarkable because it proved that Chris could offer up a groove, despite the starkness of the subject matter. "Devil Behind the Wheel" (cowritten with Matraca Berg, who also contributes golden harmony vocals) is one of those driving-your-truck-with-the-windows-rolled-down songs—insisting that you move your head in time with its steady rhythm. Likewise, the full-out rock of "Banging Away," with its rough vocals and swaying beat, is equal parts Steve Earle and John Mellencamp.

Critics hailed the literary merits of these albums: intricate plotlines, rich characterization, and a strong sense of place—qualities that once defined mainstream country music, with its timeless themes of hardship, love, and loss. From Merle Travis's classic "Dark as a Dungeon" in the 1940s to Loretta Lynn's "Coal Miner's Daughter" in the 1970s and Matraca Berg's "Strawberry Wine" in the 1990s, country music at its best has produced true literature. And while the genre has a long history of novelty songs—think June Carter and Broadway composer Frank Loesser's ditty "No Swallerin' Place" or Bobby Bare's "Drop Kick Me Jesus (through the Goalposts of Life)"—they were the exception, lighthearted and creative tunes intended to draw a good laugh. Nowadays, however, they are the norm, as mainstream country music has largely descended into one-dimensional sing-alongs about back roads (cue Luke Bryan's "Country Girl [Shake It for Me]"), beer guzzling (Toby Keith's "Get Drunk and Be Somebody"), and even body parts (Trace Adkins's "Honky Tonk Badonkadonk").

Compare these songs to "Rural Route," an artistic gem from Chris's 2006 release, *Enough Rope*. Although he sings of back roads and beer, these are incidental images; the theme itself is the loss of a physical and spiritual place: "I'd go back but I can't go home / Cause the river is up and the road is closed." And then there's "Jack Blue," a tune about a small-town hell-raiser who is "always breaking the law" and could have been the main character in a Larry Brown short story. The difference is obvious: Chris's songs are literature.

"It's you telling a story in your song," Chris says. "I call that literature to a point. I can take probably over half of my songs—if I wrote books, there would probably be a whole book or at least a bunch of short stories if you put them together. I wasn't a short story writer or I didn't write novels, but I could put them to music. I read a lot of Cormac McCarthy, William Faulkner, Elizabeth Maddox Roberts, and Chris Offutt, and they put you in a place that you knew about, but you never thought about being there until you read their book. I try to write from that place.

"I've listened to country music on and off my whole life. I don't listen to Top 40 country music anymore. I don't really think about it. I'll be switching through the channels, and I'll hear a good song every now and then. There was one period when I thought country music was really good, and that was '86 to '88—Dwight Yoakam, Patty Loveless, Steve Earle. It had a little bit of hillbilly in it, I guess. But that right there, they ain't doing that no more."

Americana, he says, is carrying on the tradition of early country music and the folk rock traditions of the 1960s and 1970s: "It's more story-oriented. And [the mainstream country industry] can't necessarily sign a fifty-year-old man who writes about shooting people, you know?"

When Chris was thirteen, his older brother introduced him to the music of John Prine. Together, they would listen to Prine's records on an elaborate stereo his brother had purchased after he went to work in the mines. "That's where I really got into music," Chris remembers. "I knew [Prine's] family was from Western Kentucky. He was a big influence on me."

The songs he heard at that turntable—Prine's epic "Paradise," about nearby Muhlenberg County, and others by Jackson Browne and Lynyrd Skynyrd—inspired him to pick up the guitar two years later. It took him ten years to get around to testing out his songwriting chops after hearing Steve Earle's debut album, *Guitar Town,* when it was released in 1986. "I'd always written songs, but they all wound up in the trash can," he says, laughing about it now. "I probably wrote over a hundred songs before I ever wrote one that stuck around."

He also worked up the nerve to perform live, playing at bars in nearby Madisonville and Henderson. But he chafed when he learned that the bar owners expected him to act as a glorified beer salesman, hawking Bud Light and Pabst Blue Ribbon from the stage in between songs. Leaving the honky-tonk circuit, he turned his attention to Nashville, which was just a two-hour drive down I-24, and inked a writing deal with Bluewater Music only a year later. During this time, he recorded a series of demos, raw performances in his trailer. The next decade saw these sessions become legendary among his hard-core Americana fans, trickling out in bootleg recordings. He finally caved to popular pressure in 2007, choosing eleven of the thirty tracks to release as *The Trailer Tapes.* Even with producer and engineer Ray Kennedy's expert polishing, the album is technically imperfect, spotlighting Chris's performance anxiety and the occasional bit of background noise. But that's not the point. *The Trailer Tapes* also showcases his development as an artist, warts and all. "At first I didn't see the appeal," he says, "but that's probably because I was too close to it."

Chris returned to the studio the following year to record *Heart of Stone,* a loud, rollicking set of songs that many call the album of his career. Embracing a full-on roots rock sound, humming with electric guitars, accordions, and fiddles, the record was more accessible and introspective than previous outings, yet it retained the stark subject matter that had become Chris's trademark. "Something to Keep Me Going" is his most radio-friendly song to date, a bittersweet number about struggling with the emotions of a breakup. Set to a midtempo rhythm, the tune boasts a rich and mellow electric guitar line that glides through its sweet spot. When *Pop Matters* released its list of the best Americana albums of 2008, it was no surprise that *Heart of Stone* was at the top. The album, critics noted, "features one great song after another, making a compelling argument that Knight's the best dang country singer more people should be listening to."

He returned to his single-wide one more time in 2009 when he released *Trailer II*, twelve more songs recorded in his cramped living room in the mid-1990s. Unlike *The Trailer Tapes*, most of these tracks had been re-recorded in the studio and had appeared on other albums. By releasing the original versions, Chris wanted to preserve "the beginning of what I do now" for his fans.

Although he long ago traded the trailer for a house built on his forty acres, Chris remains essentially the same as the young man who occupied that single-wide—unpretentious and rooted in the land of Western Kentucky. "I don't know why, but ever since I was a little kid, the land and the woods and all that were just really important," he says. "Actually, Daniel Boone was my idol, you know? I had a scrapbook—I've still got it somewhere—I kept on Daniel Boone and Kentucky history when I was in the second and third grade. It's just always been important to me. People that grow up in the country—they've got a family history, knowing what their great-grandparents and great-great-grandparents went through. There's quite a bit of family stories. They've got a sense of place. I think I've always had that."

If there's any message he hopes to send in his music, it's that "country people ain't really that dumb," he laughs. "The characters in my songs have got dignity. I think if you grew up in Kentucky you've got some kind of story to tell. People come out of the hills, and their family is having to move on to different places to provide [for themselves]. There's a lot to write about in Kentucky."

Always the prolific songwriter, Chris has produced more than an album's worth of material over the last few years and is preparing to return to the recording studio, lining up a producer and a sound engineer over the summer. But for now, he aims to finish that barn.

Essential Tracks

"House and 90 Acres"
"The River's Own"
"Rural Route"
"Here Comes the Rain"
"Enough Rope"

4

Carla Gover

Mountain Edge

Highway 66 is a two-lane, serpentine road that winds through the hills and hollers of Clay County in Eastern Kentucky, past dilapidated tobacco barns and open fields of kudzu and ironweed. Like many mountain roads, this one follows the water, its gray curves mimicking the bends and twists of the Red Bird River below, passing through the blink-and-you'll-miss-them communities of Eriline and Spurlock. Nine miles and countless potholes later, the highway ends in the small town of Oneida, population 2,627.

But more interesting than the road's final destination are its tendrils that splay out along the way, forking off into hollers with Appalachian names such as Jacks Creek and Banks' Branch. Homes of every type speckle the hillsides of these communities— trailers, cabins, clapboard shotguns, bricked ranch-style houses, even a garish McMansion or two. As these styles of homes imply, families in this area are preserving the old mountain ways to varying degrees. It was easier forty years ago, long before Facebook, iPods, and cable television became stiff competition for porch sitting, passing along family stories, and making music.

This was the backdrop of old-time musician and songwriter Carla Gover's childhood in the late 1970s, when she visited her maternal grandparents on weekends and during the summer months at the family homeplace on Banks' Branch. Although she lived only two counties away with her parents in Letcher County, there was a world of difference between the two places; Banks' Branch was a step back in time for the young girl. Her grandparents' house had burned, and they were living in a trailer with no running water, a notion that Carla found somewhat exotic. "We got the water from a spring up behind the house," she recalls. "This was actually cool, because it meant that we kept a bucket and dipper by the door for drinking, and dishpans in the sink for washing hands. As a kid, I didn't see that as an inconvenience—I thought it was fun."

She roamed the mountainside behind the trailer with her cousins, running in between the birches and redbuds, her mane of blonde hair thrashing behind her. But their buoyant play would soon turn somber as they came upon a series of rock houses. "Grandma explained that those were where our Cherokee ancestors lived, before our white ancestors came to Kentucky. [We] would pretend we lived up there and we'd gather plants from the woods to stock our pretend larders," she explains with a broad smile.

Below the trailer was a large bottom field that contained the garden, and just beyond it was Banks' Branch itself, a deep, meandering creek that Carla describes as "the only toy we needed." She and her cousins spent entire mornings and afternoons there, whiling away the time by balancing on the footbridges that spanned the branch in different spots and wading in the clear waters, hunting for crawdads with sticks and strings.

After a substantial supper of soup beans and cornbread, complemented by fresh vegetables from the garden, the family could often be found walking the holler, stopping in to visit relatives who lived nearby. An image comes to mind as Carla reminisces about these evenings: as the fading sun dribbled down through the translucent roof of beech leaves, her grandmother would express her thanks for another day by singing her favorite hymns, such as "Family Reunion" and "Just a Rose Will Do." Her plaintive voice echoed down the holler, a fitting coda to the cares of the day.

> I'll go to a beautiful garden
> At last when life's work is through.
> Don't spend your money for flowers
> Just a rose will do

Hymns and church music were among the first songs Carla remembers hearing. And because her family was affiliated with a variety of Christian denominations, she was exposed to a wide range of musical styles. "My grandmother went to Holiness, my grandfather went to an Old Regular Baptist, my mother just went to the First Baptist, and my brother went to a Methodist," she chortles. "The Holiness was my favorite music."

Carla and her grandmother often spent their Saturday nights at a one-room Pentecostal church made of gray cinder blocks that sat just off of Highway 66. She sat transfixed in the pews as the preacher strode up to the podium, cracked his Bible, and unleashed an old-time fire-and-brimstone sermon that made it sound as if the flames of hell were just outside the church's doors, whipping the congregation into a frenzy. Before long, the entire church would be engulfed in a different kind of blaze altogether— a holy fire, the preacher said. The fabled tongues from the book of Acts would descend, spreading throughout the church, and soon nearly the entire congregation would be speaking in that unknown language, some of them dancing and writhing. Shout-

Carla Gover describes Banks' Branch as the only toy she
needed as a child. (Photo courtesy of artist)

ing, they called it. An elderly woman from up the creek might feel
compelled to give a prophecy.

The impassioned theater of the experience was unforgettable,
Carla says, but what made the most impact was the music, rough

and gritty and liberating. "Most often there wouldn't be any pickers there," she remembers. "The preacher sometimes lined out the songs.* Grandma had a beautiful voice that would make the short hairs on the back of your neck stand up. It was raw and mountain as could be. I sang along."

The songs themselves and the loosely structured Holiness music tradition—in which participants felt free to repeat verses at will or even throw in an impromptu original verse—spoke to the young Carla's creative spirit. "I just always was drawn to music, whether it was played or whether it was sung," she says. "And fortunately, I was in a place where it was easy to come by. It was just all around."

Even her aunts and uncles brought their music with them from Ohio when they visited Banks' Branch, leading the family in old-time mountain songs and more modern country tunes. "My mother and grandmother liked to sing; my uncles all played. When I was growing up, it was more like the guys were all the pickers and the women were the singers. So it was kind of brave for me when I decided to play guitar."

At ten, she began taking informal lessons from a woman at church, she explains, because her uncles were not around to teach her themselves. "My mom had ten brothers and sisters, and she's the only one that stayed in Kentucky," she says. "I've always joked about how thankful I am."

Jesting though she may be, there is more than a hint of sheer honesty tucked away in the folds of her soft laughter.

Carla is standing offstage in the middle of the Mary E. Mars Gymnasium on the campus of Lincoln Memorial University, a small

---

* Lining out is a method of a cappella hymn singing in which a leader chants each line of lyrics before they are sung by the congregation. The practice is thought to have originated in England.

liberal arts college in Harrogate, Tennessee, just a few miles from the Kentucky border. The temperature in the gym is rising, compounded by the growing number of bodies and the fact that the air-conditioning is on the blink. Still, no one is complaining. The doors are flung open, allowing the occasional breeze to trickle in, carrying with it the sounds of crickets from the nearby creek.

As the musical headliner of the 2007 Mountain Heritage Literary Festival, an annual weekend gathering of Appalachian writers, Carla is right at home, conversing freely with a cadre of participants who are admiring the banjo slung over her shoulder. She fans herself with a program, listening intently as an elderly woman tells her about growing up in Clay County. "My people were from Banks' Branch," she replies, a subject she returns to later that evening onstage.

"I wrote this next song about my grandma," she tells the audience, exchanging her banjo for a guitar. "She was a mountain woman through and through." Flinging her hair back, she tweaks the instrument's tuning pegs and nods to fiddler Brett Ratliff on her left, who raises his bow and pulls out the opening bars of the midtempo tune. She grins and joins in on the guitar, along with J. T. Cure on the upright bass. As Carla rocks back and forth, her body mirroring her guitar strums, her face takes on a stoic expression as she begins to sing in the voice of her grandmother:

> Run to the spring, fetch me some water
> You be my legs, my young granddaughter
> You know I don't get around the way I used to
> Won't you do for me the things I cannot do

Even the melody seems to have been plucked out of the old garden on Banks' Branch, a tune as rich as Clay County soil. Guitar, fiddle, and bass mingle with the monotonous rhythm of tapping feet on the tarpaulin-covered floor as Carla trills the refrain: "Me

Me and the Red Bird River

Run to the spring, fetch me some water
You be my legs, my young granddaughter
You know I don't get around the way I used to
Won't you do for me the things I cannot do

Pin up my hair, there's company coming
We'd better get some biscuits in the oven
You know I'll fry this meat and when I'm through
You set the table and I'll sing a song for you

Chorus
Chief Redbird fell in the muddy water
That's the last they heard of him
I've lived my life on the banks of the river
But I never did learn to swim

Well the wild geese fly and the coal trains rattle
And the time keeps slipping on by
But me and the Red Bird River
Gonna roll on till we die

These apples here are good for frying
We'll peel the rest and put 'em up for drying
You know I can't stand to see 'em lay and spoil
Our winter's gain will be our summer's toil

Chorus

Bridge
I used to fly across these hills, run barefoot through the spring
Thought I could see the whole world, Lord, and how I'd shout
and sing

> But my running days are over and my soul is almost free
> Won't you go up on that mountain and sing one song for me
>
> We'll make our quilt from these old britches
> Now have a care and take some smaller stitches
> It's something new from something old
> To keep us warm through all the winter's cold
>
> *Chorus*

and the Red Bird River / Are gonna roll on till we die." As the last chord rings out, many of the workshop participants have begun whispering to one another: she is one of them. "She's a real writer," a redheaded poet whispers to a friend.

Carla surprises them on the next song by slipping on a pair of dance shoes and clogging wildly to a fiddle tune. Her feet are a blur, rising and falling to the music as her zebra-print skirt swishes from side to side. She is serious at first, intent on delivering a masterful performance, but that quickly transitions to a broad smile as the crowd claps along. Some holler their approval, and one man even breaks into a flat foot back near the bleachers. Carla finishes with a stomp, and the writers reward her with a standing ovation.

To conclude the show, she returns to her banjo and pitches them one final curveball—an old-time rendition of the 1980s feminist anthem "Girls Just Want to Have Fun," replete with a lively fiddle solo from Ratliff. Carla glides over the lyrics in a voice that is Jean Ritchie meets Cyndi Lauper, a soft mountain trill with a modern edge. Laughter bubbles up from the crowd, and most sing along, knowing the words by heart. This, like Carla, represents their Appalachia—an amalgam of traditional and contemporary influences that belies the notion that the region is out of touch with modern life. It's a stereotype that Carla enjoys defying, one that she has been rolling her eyes at since she was a teenager.

At age thirteen, Carla moved with her family from Letcher County to Richmond, Kentucky, after her father lost his job with a coal company. Concerned about her education, her parents enrolled her in Model Laboratory School, a semiprivate institution situated on the campus of Eastern Kentucky University. While she received a stellar education, Carla admits that she often faced discrimination due to her mountain roots and thick accent. Her initial response was to change herself. "I learned how to try to not talk like I was from the mountains because I didn't want people to think I was stupid," she sighs. "And they did."

She kept her passion for old-time music hidden as well, until one summer when she attended the Kentucky Governor's School for the Arts with other talented high school juniors and seniors. The students and faculty organized a coffeehouse for literary and musical performances, and Carla was inspired by the diversity of styles and genres. "Everybody was playing different stuff, and I got up and played traditional tunes and it was really well received. I was surprised because I had thought that everybody might laugh at me, and they were like, 'That's so cool that you learned that from your grandmother.' It gave me the courage to start sharing my background more with my peers, and the older I got, the more I realized that rather than trying to act like I wasn't from the mountains, I wanted to let people know that I *was* from the mountains and actively work to change the stereotype."

By the time she started college at the University of Kentucky a few years later, Carla had come full circle, fully embracing her mountain heritage. She majored in Appalachian studies and began pursuing her music with zest, even finding time to take up

"I wanted to let people know that I *was* from the mountains and actively work to change the stereotype." —Carla Gover (Photo courtesy of artist)

the banjo. For this endeavor, she returned to her native Letcher County for lessons with Lee Sexton, a master banjo picker whose gritty clawhammer style has been featured on the Smithsonian Folkways album *Mountain Music of Kentucky* and other traditional recordings. Sexton was born in 1927 and took up the banjo at the age of eight, so his mentoring of Carla ensured that her playing style conjures that era instead of the more refined methods of modern times. "He would always joke and say, 'There's not many women that play that hard-driving style. I bet I've learned her that,'" she recalls proudly.

A certain reverence seeps into her soft voice as she speaks of her long list of musical mentors, which includes fellow Kentuckians Sexton, fiddler and mandolin player Rich Kirby, and singer-songwriter Ron Short, along with bluegrass great Hazel Dickens and acclaimed folk singer Ginny Hawker. When Carla left the mountains for a brief stint with Footworks, a Maryland-based percussive dance and music ensemble that performs in venues around the globe, her relationship to Appalachia crystallized once and for all. "It made me realize what I had," she muses. "Then the coolest part was having those mentors to turn back to when I realized the value of it so that I could mine the vein of their experiences more deeply.

"I did a lot of work in the schools over there, and one thing that made me realize [is] this is great and all, but I want to go back home and work in the schools to try to instill pride, to change the stereotypes and encourage Appalachians to really tell their own stories instead of looking for some outside source to tell it."

Upon returning to Kentucky at age twenty-four, Carla set to work recording her first album, *Hush, My Restless Soul,* an expansive collection of songs that includes classic old-time tunes ("Sweet Fern," "Your Long Journey"), an African American gospel number ("God's Not Dead"), and a moving cover of the Hazel Dickens classic "Don't Put Her Down (You Helped Put Her There)." She also threw in a few original compositions, including the title track, a starkly produced a cappella hymn, reminiscent of Jean Ritchie's "Now Is the Cool of the Day," that combines the beauty of the natural world with a quiet, abiding faith.

While recording *Hush, My Restless Soul,* Carla recruited many of the musicians she had met in Maryland to play on the album. One of them, she remembers, suggested that she pitch it to Appalshop, the respected nonprofit media collective based in Whitesburg, Kentucky, that produces music, original films, theatrical productions, radio shows, and photography. She took the advice and submitted her partially completed record to the organization's famous June Appal Recordings folk label. June Appal's decision to help her finish the album fulfilled a childhood aspiration. Growing up in Letcher County, near Appalshop, she says, "I used to . . . dream that I would have an album on June Appal one day."

The record's release meant more tour dates for Carla, and she became a regular presence on the old-time and folk festival circuits. The following year, she reconnected with Mitch Barrett, a folksinger from Madison County whom she had met at a festival a few years back. The pair married and formed a duo, Zoe Speaks, merging their respective sounds through original songs. "Mitch had a really traditional background in terms of singing in church and stuff. He just had never been drawn to learn the instrumental stuff like I had. But [his] singing was really old-timey, [and] obviously he was drawing on his lessons from Neil Young and John Prine. I had all that, too, so it was an easy fit. I think it made us more appealing to a broader audience. It grew very organically."

Their debut album, *Pearl,* released in 2000, capitalized on their distinct harmonies and blend of genres. Songs such as "Summerflight" and "Angel Wings" embrace a more contemporary folk sound, while others like "Money's Our God" and "Old Pete" hear-ken back to their old-time roots. The duo began touring full-time in a large van with their two daughters in tow, and the following year saw Carla win the Chris Austin Songwriting Contest at the popular Merlefest in North Carolina.

In 2002 Carla and Mitch released *Birds Fly South,* a record that continued their mix of old and new and paid tribute to Carla's grandmother with a haunting a cappella rendition of "Just a Rose Will Do." Further nods to tradition included the old hymn "Family Reunion" and a cover of the English ballad "Barbry Ellen," featuring a sparkling lead vocal turn by Carla. Originals such as "I Believe," a song about shirking one's strict religious upbringing for a more generous spirituality, showcased a more contemporary sound, but the pair's gritty reworking of the traditional mountain song "Shady Grove" perhaps best defined their music. Recast as a tale of an interracial relationship, the tune detailed the couple's longing to make their love public, a desire that cannot be fulfilled due to their community's prejudices.

Such fresh explorations of life in modern Appalachia resonated with audiences and music critics throughout the country. "Their spare arrangements and unwavering harmonies evoke Gillian Welch and David Rawlings (and generations of singers before them)," wrote *Acoustic Guitar* magazine, which also dubbed Carla "one of the thirty essential artists of the next generation." The pair turned in acclaimed performances at Merlefest and the Kerrville Folk Festival, and a prestigious gig on the Millennium Stage in the Grand Foyer of the John F. Kennedy Center for the Performing Arts in Washington, D.C.

As much as they loved the road, Carla says there was no comparison when it came to performing before a home-state audience. "I'm always so glad to come back to a Kentucky audience after I've been somewhere else because there's this enthusiasm you can even feel as a performer onstage. People nod their heads, they tap their feet, they clap their hands, they go *woo* way more often than people in most other parts of the world. People love it so much, and that's essentially it."

In 2005 Carla and Mitch put their many years of experience performing at festivals to good use by founding the Clear Creek Festival. Held each Labor Day weekend in a copse of trees on a mountainside near the arts town of Berea, the festival has become something of a cultural institution in the state, featuring roots music, theater, dance, film, art installations, and spoken-word performances by some of the region's best-known artists.

Despite their creative synergy, Carla and Mitch's marriage had run out of steam by 2008, when they released the buoyant *Drop in the Bucket,* their swan song as a duo. Described in its press kit as a "cosmic possum" production—borrowing a term coined by Tennessee poet Jane Hicks to describe socially enlightened Appalachians who continue to embrace their mountain roots—the album features "Sacred Yard," a meditation on creation, and the title track, an up-tempo number about social justice that honors pioneers including Rosa Parks, Mohandas Gandhi, and Mother Teresa. But the emotional centerpiece of the album is the last track, "Me and the Red Bird River."

Although the song is a tribute to her grandmother, Carla had other intentions for it as well. "I'd been at Merlefest," she says, "and I heard lots of great music there, but there were so many bands that were playing old-time music and singing these songs about meth dealers or people murdered and thinking they were being so Appalachian, but they weren't even from there. And I started that song in a motel room thinking, 'You know, I want to write a song about what it was really like for me to grow up in Eastern Kentucky [without] all these romanticized [notions], either in a quaint, poetic way or a violent, fugitive, drinking, drug-doing kind of way.' That was my way of saying, 'This is where I'm from.'"

The Cowan Community Center in Whitesburg is humming with activity on a warm morning in late June. Although this is the first day of the annual Cowan Creek Music School, the atmosphere is more like that of a family reunion. People of all ages trickle in with instrument cases slung over their shoulders or dangling from their hands—guitars, fiddles, banjos, autoharps. They gather in small groups and start up excited conversations, catching up on the past year's events before being interrupted by someone else demanding a hug.

"Look at you," exclaims a delighted woman to a young towheaded boy with a fiddle. He grins and blushes in response. "You've grown so much!"

Carla is here in the middle of the throng, hugging necks and dispensing compliments on everything from instruments to shoes. Later, she leads a workshop for a packed audience in a cramped classroom, strumming her guitar and singing one of her own songs to illustrate a point. She is comfortable as a teacher, having conducted numerous music and dance workshops in elementary and high schools throughout the state in an effort to teach cultural heritage skills.

"You never know when you touch that one kid," she says softly. "I mean, I know it sounds like a cliché, but I remember just about every assembly we ever had at my school. Just having one person stand up and say, 'This is really cool that you're from here; you're so lucky to have all this tradition and information and folklore around you. Take advantage of it.' Just one person reframing it and helping them look at it in a different way than TV, movies, and in some instances teachers and parents have taught them to look at it. It's really important, and I feel strongly about it. I've been doing this long enough that I've actually gotten e-mails [saying], 'You came to my school twelve years ago and I just want you to know that I'm playing music today.' It's pretty cool when you get to see that kind of thing."

Carla connects her music and cultural education activities with what she sees as a growing hunger for more authentic ways of living across the country—"searching for roots," as she calls it. She muses at length about people who haunt antique malls and flea markets looking for old furniture and housewares, and how some even distress new tables in an effort to make them pass for heirlooms. Roots music is flourishing in this environment, she says, describing it as "an interactive forum."

In 2010 Carla released her first solo album in fifteen years. A spirited ensemble of songs, *Gypsy Ways* is her most blatant fusion of old-time and modern sounds, boasting traditional tunes like "Blackjack Davy" and her take on the English ballad "Lady Isabell and the Elfin Knight," alongside fan favorite "Girls Just Want to Have Fun," with its vibrant banjo licks.

Now remarried and with a new baby, Carla is planning to return to the studio for a concept album devoted to Appalachian archetypes. Her writing process, she says, consists of embedding symbols within the lyrics. "One of the things I've done so far is starting a word and image bank. It's got iron skillets and corn for dinner, pocketknives and overalls, banjos and jack corn, rivers and just all these things that to me symbolize different aspects of the culture. It's going to have a lot of Kentucky."

When pressed to explain how she manages to bridge such divides—traditional and modern, old-time and contemporary folk—Carla shrugs, replying that she tries not to overthink it. "I just do what I want to do or what I feel like doing without worrying so much about whether it's old or new," she explains, a quiet determination permeating her voice. "Because music is like that—it crosses borders and boundaries, and it's fluid."

Essential Tracks

"Hush, My Restless Soul"
"Me and the Red Bird River" (Zoe Speaks)
"Girls Just Want to Have Fun"
"When I Want Lovin' (Baby I Want You)"
"One Small Bird" (Zoe Speaks)

5

Kevin Harris

Freedom Doxology

doxology: a usually liturgical expression of praise to God.
—*Merriam-Webster's Collegiate Dictionary*

The metal cross on the lone turret of Greater Liberty Baptist Church shimmers in the midmorning sun, a beacon above the clapboard homes and shotgun houses that line either side of Chestnut Street in Lexington's East End. It is a handsome building, red brick trimmed with white stone arches over the windows. A curved garden area sits in front, between the twin sets of steps leading to the entrances. On the ridgeline of the black-shingled roof, a row of black crows roosts, oblivious to the clusters of people ambling up the sidewalk and stairs into the church.

Inside the sanctuary, an organ swells the call to worship as the choir pulls the old spiritual "Last Day of the Week" out of its repertoire. Many in the congregation stand, clapping along and swaying back and forth. A woman in the second pew lifts her hands toward the vaulted ceiling, her flamboyant hat moving nary an inch as she inclines her head in the same direction. "Praise Jesus," people call out throughout the sanctuary. "Thank you, Lord," the bishop shouts as he kicks up his leg in a dance of praise before approaching the microphone for a passionate sermonette.

A few moments later, the Clark Sisters take the stage. Known throughout the community for their vocal prowess, they do not disappoint this morning, leading the crowd in a rendition of "His Eye Is on the Sparrow" so powerful that the stained glass windows seem to rattle in their lead casings.

Midway down the left side of the room, a small boy sits in a pew, hands folded in his lap, taking it all in. He marvels at the whine of the organ, takes in the slurs and sevenths from the piano player, old blues licks that have seeped in from the world outside. His mother is singing harmony beside him. She is standing, her eyes closed tight, intent on worshipping. Despite her focus on heavenly things, she feels him looking at her. She glances down and catches him smiling. He returns to the music.

Kevin Harris strides into the Central Square location of Starbucks in Cambridge, Massachusetts, ready for a cup of coffee. He has spent the last few weeks prepping for his record release party scheduled for tonight at Scullers, one of Boston's premier jazz clubs, and desperately needs a pick-me-up to help propel him across the finish line. Even though it's an early afternoon in late May, a chill has descended on the city. A brisk wind from the nearby Charles River whips through the streets. In defiance of the temperature, a man walks by on the sidewalk licking a chocolate ice cream cone.

Coffee in hand, Kevin leans back in his chair, intent on relaxing before the sound check and show that will follow. He chats about his adopted city of twelve years, of its importance to American history and the 2.5-mile Freedom Trail, an official walking tour of Boston's most famous historical landmarks. But he soon shifts gears to modern Beantown, with its educational centers, scores of ethnic restaurants, and sophisticated music scene.

"There's a musicianship, an artistry, here on the streets of Boston," he says, wrapping his long, slender fingers around the paper cup. "You see people walking up and down the sidewalk with guitars on their backs. Basses, drums. That was what drew me in."

It took some prodding from a cousin who was already living here to convince Kevin to move from Kentucky in 1998. He was twenty-three and intent on studying jazz piano after teaching music for a couple of years following his graduation from Morehead State University in Eastern Kentucky. His cousin had sent him an application from the New England Conservatory of Music. "He [was] saying, 'I can't think of any jazz clubs in Kentucky that just support playing. But there are jazz clubs up here. Jazz schools. I'm sending you an application. You are going to see the price of the school, and I don't want you to be intimidated. Don't worry about it. Just trust me.' And I did."

Kevin was accepted following a nerve-racking audition and began scurrying to classes, private lessons, and his work-study position in the Information Technology Department. But to supple-

The Magic of Jazz

Kevin can trace his entire musical philosophy back to the moment he heard his junior high school band director play "Georgia on My Mind" on the piano. "He played the tune, then he started to improvise a bit, then he came back to it," he says. "And that transition, being able to transform something like that, and then come back—it's like [being] a magician."

His years onstage have given him even greater insight into that process: "I learned that you are not only doing that with the tune, you're doing that with your audience, too. You're doing that with yourself, and you kind of transform—going somewhere and coming back and making everything connect."

ment his formal training, he began frequenting jazz clubs around the city, where he was exposed to a fusion of musical styles—rhythms imported from Cuba, Peru, and Venezuela—that made a deep impression. Where before he had been studying music primarily to become a teacher, his time spent in Boston's jazz clubs led him to refocus on his own musicianship.

"That's a different education," he muses. "I think that's what woke me up—and continues to wake me up. Those musicians knew all the tunes, no matter what you called. I would see jam sessions—these guys who knew all the tunes and kind of gave each other a hard time when they weren't all there. If you don't know your stuff when you get up there, thinking you are going to play—'It's nothing personal, but go home and practice. Sorry man,' they'll tell you. 'Yeah, that was nice. You got easy rhythm, but I didn't hear the change.' In other words, 'You don't know the song.' And they were telling me that right off the bat."

He upped his game at the piano, and soon he was playing his own gigs in the same clubs he had once been sent home from. When he graduated in 2000 with a master's degree in jazz piano performance, Kevin set to work on his first album, a set of five songs titled *Patient Harvest*. He also began teaching music workshops throughout Boston with Arts in Progress, a now defunct nonprofit arts advocacy organization that mentored and educated youth throughout the city, and took a job with the Cambridge Friends School as the institution's jazz band director.

During this time, Kevin returned to Kentucky periodically through his work with Arts in Progress, which was partnering with an agency in Louisville called New Performing Arts to send a diverse sampling of artists to far-flung areas of the state. "That always felt good, connecting me to a part of Kentucky that I didn't know," he recalls. "I grew up in Lexington, and I didn't get around to see a lot of Kentucky, so that left an impression on me. The

Kevin Harris, at home with the keys. (Photo courtesy of artist)

more of Kentucky I saw, the more I appreciated where I was coming from."

In between teaching and music gigs, Kevin was composing material for a new recording project. Released in 2007, *The Butterfly Chronicles* features what *Jazz Times* called his "sparse style and . . . gentle touch" on the keys. For his first full-length album, Kevin gave a nod to his Kentucky roots on the first track, a thirty-six-second piano intro under a voice mail from his brother: "Kevin Harris, we love you, man. Your family loves you. We know you love us. Our thoughts and prayers are always with you. You're a successful and talented individual. Continue to do good things."

A perfectly timed hesitation follows. "And I expect to be paid for that nice commentary." Laughter erupts in the background.

The inclusion of this personal message sets the stage for the rest of *The Butterfly Chronicles,* which kicks off with "Strut Bucket" and its groove-inflected piano and swinging drums.

"Butterfly" is another standout track, a ruminative, straightforward ballad that showcases Kevin's melodic prowess and masterful touch on the keys.

The artistic growth demonstrated on the album is substantial, a direct result of the countless gigs and workshops he completed in the years between *Patient Harvest* and *The Butterfly Chronicles*. He explains this by turning to the outside world as a metaphor. "I'm really big into slow, meaningful progress. The way a tree grows. The way nature acts." A key part of his development, he says, was giving the record "an accessible vibe" by making the melodies less showy.

His follow-up, *Freedom Doxology,* was released a year later under the name of the Kevin Harris Project and offered a more sophisticated sound and showcase of his talents, using odd meters and advanced harmonies. "The songs are longer, more thorough—like going through different personalities and spirits within one song," he says. "There's ups, there's downs." Kevin grooves his way through tunes like "The Brown Hornet," with its rhythmic bounce, and "Pass the Hot Sauce," in which his fingers seem to glide over the keys. The mood turns introspective and somber on the title track, an intense song Kevin has referred to in interviews as "a form of musical worship."

"It starts off—it's got this low rumble. It's that same rumble that happens when the preacher at church starts, 'And Moses said,'" he intones, mimicking an African American minister's cadence. "There's the rumble going on, this one note, and the organ's on it, the bass player is on it. I'm doing that with my left hand. It's a musical and spiritual connection. It's the blues. It's an expression of *this is where I'm coming from.* It's almost liberating when I play that song. If I'm halfway through a concert and I'm feeling nervous or a little antsy about how things are going, I play that song. It calms me down, reminds me who I am. Nothing about it is fancy or fast. It just speaks to where I come from, and actually to where I'm going. It has to do with those conversations that people have but the real topic is unsaid. A lot of times before I play that song, we talk about rhythm. We'll talk about maybe what slaves didn't get to talk about. Maybe the things that haven't been said over the years—you know, Maya Angelou has said that phrase, 'we've already been paid for.' And in a way I feel like that song is dedicated to a lot of folks who paved the way for me. It's like a thank you. It's a way to speak for them." He pauses and grins, taking a swig of coffee. "There's a lot there."

When Kevin returns the paper cup to the table, he does not let go. His willowy fingers maintain their grip, further emphasizing the gravity of his soliloquy. I study them for a moment, silently, marveling at their strength, realizing that the melodies they play can go to places mere lyrics cannot.

Like other forms of roots music, jazz is a language, communicating ideas and emotions through vocals, the dissonance of piano keys, and a radical bass line. But Kevin's variety of instrumental jazz takes this concept to a higher plane—the absence of lyrics places the music front and center, requiring the song's melody and arrangement to communicate its meaning.

"And Moses said," the piano growls, its low voice choked with emotion.

"We've already been paid for," the crashing cymbals reply.

This jazz is liturgy.

"As long as I could remember there has always been singing," Kevin says of his childhood in the North End of Lexington. "Somebody's foot was always tapping, somebody was always swaying, and I think that's just become a part of me."

Each morning, he would wake up to the sounds of his mother's resonant voice trickling in from the kitchen, usually singing a gospel number like "Amazing Grace" or "Take My Hand, Precious Lord." His musical education continued as the day went on, with his mother playing R&B records by Sam Cooke, Nat King Cole, and Ray Charles; Motown artists such as the Temptations and Stevie Wonder; and gospel albums by the Staple Singers and James Cleveland.

On Sundays, these sounds were supplemented by the live music he heard from the pews at Greater Liberty Baptist Church. The music of the black church, he says, was intoxicating and taught him how to discern authenticity in music. "It's hard to describe," he explains. "So many feelings. We got the experience every Sunday. It taught me what music is. It gave me that fundamental definition of what music should feel like. And for somebody who has the experience, to grow up experiencing that, then you go to a show and it ain't happening, you know right away, because it is in your blood. You turn on *American Idol* or something like that [and] you have to wait until the very end to find somebody that sounds like what you grew up with, or else you are wasting your time. It's the feeling of [your] first time listening to Aretha Franklin."

Kevin started playing the trumpet around the age of eight, and his mother often found him out in the garage pantomiming to Louis Armstrong records. But that instrument didn't stick, and he set his sights on the piano after hearing his junior high school band director play "Georgia on My Mind." "The way he played that song," Kevin smiles and shakes his head. "I knew I wanted to play the piano like that. And I had my first piano lesson—I think maybe after about two or three lessons he gave me that song and I learned it by ear. And from then on, it was piano, piano, just wanting to play by ear."

But in the middle of his musical incarnation, tragedy struck when his father died suddenly of a stroke at age forty. It was one of those unexplainable deaths—his father was in good shape, jogged

"These blues ideas are the same ones that are going on in the church. . . .
The bending of those notes—it's a very African thing." —Kevin Harris
(Photo courtesy of artist)

regularly, and watched his diet. Twenty-five years later, Kevin's
loss is still palpable. "He never really heard me play piano," he
says softly, staring out the window on to Prospect Street.

Although he wasn't aware of it at the time, Kevin explains that
he acted out his grief at the keyboard, practicing at the family's
brown-lacquered upright Baldwin for hours on end, often into the
night. "I remember my mother giving me some rules," he chuckles, "because I would get on early, and that would drive her crazy."

Soon, he began to connect the scales he was practicing to the
music of the black church. "It all came to life—these blues ideas
are the same ones that are going on in the church, the same ones
that are being sung. The bending of those notes—it's a very African thing."

He also intuitively understood the political origins of the music, that it had been birthed out of poverty and adversity. "Grow-

ing up there on the North End of Lexington, it [was] a lot of poor black folks and a lot of poor white folks, so we were a community to ourselves in my opinion. Even today you go back to the South End of Lexington, and it's like a whole other city. I didn't have any friends that grew up on the South End. I didn't know anybody that owned a horse," he notes mischievously, grinning from ear to ear. "I had an uncle who had a farm—I take that back. He had a farm, and he had a pony. We got to ride it. But the whole status definition, it just wasn't a part of my world."

Even with this socioeconomic background, Kevin was puzzled when he was first introduced to jazz during his college years at Morehead. Steeped in gospel and the blues, he says that jazz "wasn't home base for me." When a friend gave him an album by jazz pianist and pioneer Thelonious Monk, his first reaction was confusion: who is this? He laughs in recollection but admits he was intrigued, especially by the more blues-influenced tunes that reminded him of Sunday mornings at Greater Liberty Baptist Church. Soon he was devouring albums by Charlie Parker, Sonny Rollins, and Duke Ellington, as well as discovering Kentucky's rich jazz heritage as the birthplace of legendary vibraphonist Lionel Hampton and vocalist Helen Humes.

Pivotal in his musical education was Jay Flippin, a Morehead professor whom Kevin refers to as "the piano Zeus of Kentucky." He credits Flippin with helping him to connect the dots between classical and jazz and other genres of roots music. "He would sit down and show me, 'You are learning Bach, how does that relate to what Buddy Holly's doing? You see the way he's improvising here?' He would call Bach the first jazz musician, drawing the bigger picture of music in general."

It's a teaching style that Kevin has come to rely on in his classroom at the Cambridge Friends School and as an assistant professor at the renowned Berklee School of Music. Although he teaches his younger students how to read music, he also requires them to record what he plays in class so they can learn music by ear. His instructions to his older students are simple: "Get out and play. Play with people. There is a part of your schooling that you get in the classroom, and then there's a little bit more of the real-world schooling that you get outside of that classroom. And I'm a firm believer in that. That's where you learn music."

In the process, he hopes to instill in his students a certain pride that they are part of an exclusively American genre of roots music, a realization that he continues to marvel at, even as a professional musician. "Jazz is an American art form. I'm connected to that. That's what I'm a part of. And whether at the root of that is anger, I'm not sure. It could be. Sadness—it could be. I don't know; that's going really deep. But there's something there that I love being associated with."

The white electric sign on the corner of the Doubletree Guest Suites glows in the evening sunset, a beacon above the sculling crew team practicing on the Charles River. They zip under the River Street Bridge following the current, their oars rowing in perfect rhythm. The cry of the coxswain pierces the roar of traffic on the bridge: "Keep at it!"

Inside the Doubletree, Scullers Jazz Club is quickly filling to capacity. Members of the waitstaff twist and turn their bodies among the tables in an effort to collect drink and dinner orders. Glasses of Cabernet and Riesling begin to dot the linen-covered tables, quickly followed by steaming bowls of clam chowder and plates of pan-seared Atlantic salmon. The frenzied din turns to quiet conversation as food and drink are consumed, transitioning to silence when the musicians take the stage.

Kevin slides onto the bench of the black-lacquered baby grand piano, adjusting the microphone on its tripod stand. "How are you all doing tonight?" he asks, prompting a round of applause. "Welcome to our record release party."

Many in the audience have already picked up a copy of the album from the merchandise table in the foyer, and some of them hold up its multicolored checked cover in response. *Chapters* is a complex album devoted to improvisation. While most tracks are originals, Kevin has included new arrangements of songs by three of his musical heroes: Thelonious Monk, John Coltrane, and Charlie Parker.

He sounds the call to listen on the keys, a deep rumble that transitions into an up-tempo groove sustained by the drums and bass. Around the room, many bob their heads in time to the music, in between sips of wine. Kevin glides effortlessly through his set list, made up largely of songs from the new album, including the diverse movements of "The Americas" and the laid-back swing of "Buy Ya Books."

By the end of the set list he is grinning broadly, his teeth gleaming under the spotlights. His expression turns serious, though, as he starts the last song with a low rumble on the keys, a reverberation that grows so powerful that the wine glasses seem to rattle on the tables. The cymbals crash around the note, pulling the crowd even further into his "Freedom Doxology." Kevin moves into the old blues licks that have been a part of his musical life since he was a boy in the pew of Greater Liberty Baptist Church—slurs and sevenths and diminished triads.

His mother is seated at a table front and center, her eyes glued to her son. Despite his focus on the music, he feels her looking at him. He glances down and catches her smiling.

He returns to the music.

Essential Tracks

"Strut Bucket"
"Butterfly"
"Journey's End"
"Freedom Doxology"
"The Americas"

6

Joan Osborne

Brooklyn Meets Appalachia

Salyersville, Kentucky. Late October 1937. The surrounding mountains are afire with the rich hues of dying leaves that rustle and flap in the crisp breeze. Some break off and flail through the air before descending to speckle the surface of the Licking River.

Imagine this: Somewhere just outside of town—perhaps deep in some lonesome holler—a young, dark-haired man wearing a tweed suit sits with his new bride in the parlor of a simple but tidy home. The mountain woman who lives there is not used to so much attention. Nell Hampton is likely suspicious of this couple at first, employees of the federal Works Progress Administration who want to record her singing folk songs. But Alan and Elizabeth Lomax are persuasive, and she finally acquiesces.

"I believe I'll sing 'The Airplane Ride,'" she says. After studying on it for a minute, she rears back and lets loose a weathered, nasally warble:

> So one of these nights at about twelve o'clock
> This old world's going to reel and rock
> Saints will tremble and cry for pain
> For the Lord's gonna come in his heavenly airplane.

As Hampton belts out the entire song, the Lomaxes lock eyes, confident that they are preserving something exceptional. When she finishes, they thank Hampton for her time and depart.

Nearly sixty years later, another Kentuckian, living miles away in New York City, hears the crackling recording of Hampton's song and is transfixed. She hums it as she waits on the subway platform, her untamed mane of sandy hair lifted by the gust of the train as it pulls into the station. When she goes into the studio to record her debut album, Joan Osborne carries it along with her as a talisman, sharing it with her producer and the other musicians.

Her mind wanders back to the almost fairy-tale quality of Hampton's tune as she records "One of Us," freshly written by a songwriting partner. It poses a simple, childlike question: "What if God was one of us?" Sensing the connection, they add a sample of the Lomax recording to the beginning of the track. Hampton's lone, craggy voice reverberates through the studio before transitioning to the twang of an electric guitar, backed up by the steady *rat-a-tat* of a high hat. The music builds in intensity, becoming more fervent and pulsing before breaking into an all-out groove. Then, that remarkable voice, among the finest of her generation: first in the form of ad-libbed wail, then launching into the lyrics with an innocent, disarming delivery.

The song resonated with music fans of all stripes when it was released to critical acclaim in 1995 as the lead single from the album *Relish*. Accompanied by a captivating video that featured shots of Coney Island alternating with Joan singing directly into the camera, "One of Us" vaulted to number four on the *Billboard* Hot 100. *Relish* was certified triple platinum the following year, eventually selling more than five million copies. Propelled by the success of the single and the follow-up hits "Right Hand Man" and "St. Teresa," Joan garnered an astounding six Grammy nominations, including Best Female Pop Vocal Performance, Record of the Year, and Song of the Year for "One of Us."

"Osborne astutely conflates the sacred and profane," *Rolling Stone* observed in an attempt to explain her widespread appeal. "What's especially winning about the woman is her range: sexy and earnest, her voice, all on its own, conveys whole choirs of feelings." This is an astute and lyrical description, but it misses the mark.

The brilliance of Joan's instrument lies not just in its emotional depth—although that quality would surely have to be measured in fathoms. If one could distill that extraordinary voice, it would be equal parts Appalachian folk, Ohio River blues, rural country, and urban gospel—separate mixtures of a whole known as Kentucky—laced with a healthy dose of sheer New York moxie.

Music preservation takes many forms. Sometimes it requires a trek into the mountains with a recording device. But more often it entails an outward migration, armed only with a strong sense of self and one hell of a voice to sing with.

It's early May in New York, but already the city is baking, its oven of concrete and steel preheating for the coming summer. On Atlantic Avenue, in the thriving Boerum Hill neighborhood of Brooklyn, the keeper of a trendy boutique pauses as she dresses a mannequin on the sidewalk, gathering and lifting her long hair to fan her neck. Just a few doors down, the patio of the Bedouin Tent Restaurant remains remarkably cool, a leafy respite enclosed by a tall, wooden stockade fence.

"This is a great little spot," Joan says over her lunch of spicy lamb and hummus. After living in her adopted hometown for nearly twenty-five years, she undoubtedly knows many such places. New York is her turf, the city where she came of age personally and artistically after moving here from Anchorage, Kentucky, to study filmmaking at New York University in the 1980s.

Her relationship with the skyscrapers and parks and trains and people of the Big Apple has been so enduring that she devoted an entire album to celebrating its spiritual significance.

Released in late 2008, *Little Wild One* was hailed by critics as a return to form for the acclaimed singer. Her seventh studio album, it reads like a collection of short stories. On the opening track, a soaring paean to New York's spirit titled "Hallelujah in the City," Joan name-checks a string of neighborhoods in her soulful tones: Riverside Drive, Brooklyn, Chelsea, Battery Park, Morningside Heights.

"The whole experience with 9/11 shocked me back into an appreciation for the city," she explains. "I started to do things I hadn't done in a while, like take the train to a stop in Queens where I'd never been before and just get out and walk around and look."

Her newfound sense of place was sparked in part by revisiting the work of one of New York's greatest poets, Walt Whitman. "There's something about the urban experience and the spirituality of [it] that he really nails in a way that I was trying to capture somehow. There is something about living in a great city like this that is the opposite of alienating. You're rubbing up against everybody all the time so you have these opportunities for just moments of recognition of your shared humanity, whether it's giving your seat to somebody on the train or just these small little moments with somebody you've never seen before and you're never going to see again."

In "Cathedrals," Joan again evokes multiple dimensions of the city's environment as she sings of surveillance cameras and the deep hollows carved out by skyscrapers:

In the cathedrals of New York and Rome
There is a feeling that you should just go home
And spend a lifetime finding out just where that is

Like many expatriates, particularly those of the artistic persuasion, the question of home is one that occasionally weighs on Joan's mind: Is home the place of one's birth, or is it where one ultimately chooses to settle? Is it a physical geography, or is it a spiritual plane? New York or Kentucky?

Throughout her career, Joan has merged the two in her music, even going so far as to bill *Little Wild One* as "Brooklyn meets Appalachia in earnest." This melding of cultures is part of her vision as an artist, she explains. "Any time I like [a form of music] I try to dig deeper and deeper and find the source of it, whether it's Sufi music from Pakistan or Appalachian murder ballads, and I tend to find that there's a lot of similarities in it. It seems like people in different cultures and places discover the same thing really."

Such parallels hold true even when restricted to more domestic spheres. Despite the numerous contrasts in their respective cultures, New York and Kentucky share an important elemental quality: historically, both have been hotbeds of traditional music, a fact that Joan learned when she arrived in New York with little knowledge of roots genres. It was there, in the blues clubs of Greenwich Village and the record stores of Bleecker Street, that she cultivated her expansive knowledge of Americana music.

Migrating to Gotham was a daunting prospect for the young girl from Anchorage whose family never locked the doors and knew everyone in the sleepy village of 2,000 residents. Only a twenty-minute drive from downtown Louisville, Anchorage provided Joan with what she calls an "uninhibited childhood" spent building tree forts in the woods and singing harmonies to John Denver and Elvis Presley records with her five siblings.

"I was not somebody who had this picture in my mind: oh, New York City is the place that you have to come, to make it," she explains. "It was simply because the college that had the best program [and] that I liked the most was in New York." Joan pauses

"I need to tell the truth to myself before I can tell it to anyone else."
—Joan Osborne (Photo by Thorston Roth)

for a bite of food and then laughs, "But then, of course, New York City is not an afterthought of a place."

Initially, she found New York overwhelming, but she quickly adjusted and made an intuitive realization. "There's something about it that felt like almost an equalization of pressure in a way.

The inside of my mind was always so ringing with all these ideas and thoughts and notions, and here was a place where the outside of me was in sync with the inside of me. I felt very much at home."

With Greenwich Village as her backdrop, Joan began working odd jobs to fund her college education, sometimes even taking a leave from classes to put in more hours and save money for tuition. On a rare night off, a friend persuaded her to accompany him to a blues bar called the Abilene Café. "We got there after the band had finished, but the piano player was still playing," she recalls. "My friend dared me to go up and sing, and said he would buy the beers if I did."

She took him up on the offer, performing Billie Holiday's classic "God Bless the Child" and impressing the pianist enough to invite her to sing at the bar's weekly open-mike night. Although Joan calls her initial forays onto New York stages "terrifying," she was also intrigued by the challenge. "I didn't have any other creative outlets at the time, not being in school," she explains. "There was something about it that really grabbed me, and I was able to slowly but surely discover that there was this whole scene and community of people doing this kind of music."

That music was pure Americana—what Joan calls "that huge, deep, taproot stuff," which stood in stark contrast to the popular and classical music that had permeated her childhood home, where her Catholic family members had tended to internalize their feelings. Roots music, with its primal emotions, captivated her. "I just fell in love with it," she smiles. "The fact that this music was so emotional and the style of singing was so passionate, it really grabbed me."

Instead of paying her tuition at NYU, Joan was soon shelling out funds for a nontraditional education at record shops in the Village, discovering seminal recordings by Howlin' Wolf, Etta James, Hank Williams, and the Louvin Brothers. "That was my music school. I wanted the raw music and experience, whether it was gospel or blues or country or soul or whatever it was. That's what appealed to me, and that's what I wanted to learn about."

She soon graduated from singing one or two songs at open mikes to performing entire sets at small clubs in the city once a month. These shows steadily increased in number over the next few years, and before long, singing had become a full-time vocation, with Joan playing concerts five nights a week in New York and traveling to venues in Philadelphia and Washington, D.C. By this time, she had developed a regional reputation and caught the attention of record producer Rick Chertoff, who was responsible for signing her to a record contract with Mercury, a major label.

Singing the Blues

"Blues music rescued me," Joan says of her latest album, *Bring It On Home,* released in March 2012. "I knew that, someday, when the time was right and my voice was ready, I wanted to make a recording like the one you're holding now."

With stunning vocals that alternate from down-in-the-gutter soul to frenzied blues grooves, *Bring It On Home* features tracks made famous by R&B greats including Ray Charles, Muddy Waters, Otis Redding, and Ike and Tina Turner. "When I began to sing in New York City in my early twenties," Joan confesses, "I wanted nothing more than to model myself on these people, to inhabit the music as they did in some small way."

On "Shake Your Hips," the album's lead track, Joan proves that there is nothing small about her adaptations. Starting off "nice and easy" in the vein of Tina Turner, she slowly builds her voice to a feverish climax, her howl of "Well ain't that eeeaaaaasy now?" setting off a blare of drums, guitars, organ, and harmonica.

"Blues artists allowed me to find and express my own depths," Joan says of her musical education. *Bring It On Home* makes it obvious that they also enabled her to soar.

"I did not have the kind of success story where I was singing in a little club one day and the next day some big producer discovered me and made me a star," she recalls. "It took a long time."

After the universal acclaim of *Relish,* Joan took some time to regroup before recording her sophomore album, *Righteous Love.* While it did not attain the same level of commercial or critical success, it proved that she was in it for the long haul, committed to her art. A well-received record of classic soul covers titled *How Sweet It Is* followed, with Joan subsequently turning in jaw-dropping performances with her covers of "(Love Is Like a) Heat Wave" and "What Becomes of the Brokenhearted" in the documentary *Standing in the Shadows of Motown.*

Coming from small-town Kentucky, Joan says the level of success she achieved was unimaginable. "There's something about growing up in the place that I did where the notion of being some sort of internationally recognized person was just. . . ." She trails off and shakes her head. "You might as well have thought that you were going to go live on the moon. It was just so out of reach, and if I had talked about any ambitions that I might have had, I would have been afraid people would laugh and say, 'Oh, who do you think you are?'"

The Catholic Church essentially posed that question to the young Joan when she voiced an ambition to become a priest. When her parents informed her that her goal was impossible due to her gender, Joan says she became "incensed" and began to question her family's faith. "I smelled a rat early on. I think that might have been the first moment of rebellion [for me]. I just sensed that that was really unfair and that I was as smart [as] if not smarter than my brothers and could do anything they could do. I just didn't get that."

This instance of discrimination led Joan to openly question church doctrine, and at the age of nine she informed her parents that she would no longer attend Mass. "My poor mom," she groans. "I remember to this day the very moment when she was trying to get all six of us dressed and in the car to get us to church on time, and I just really dug in my heels and said, 'I'm not going. I don't understand that. I don't think this is true.' So they just left me to stay at home."

She laughs, long and low, conjuring the image of her younger self in her mind. "My poor mom," she says again. "Telling that story as a mom myself, I just see it from a whole different angle now—trying to get this bratty kid in the car with a screaming baby on [her] hip."

Her religious stance can also be seen as an attempt to carve out her own personal space in a large family. As the second eldest child, Joan became a surrogate parent to her younger brothers and sisters, helping her mother break up fights, change diapers, and make lunches. It is no wonder, then, that she savored retreating to the woods behind the family home, talking to the birds as they sang to one another in the trees. She credits these experiences with preparing her for her future life as an artist.

"There is a depth of familiarity that I remember having as a child growing up in Kentucky," she recalls, "surrounded by nature and having the freedom to roam around and the space and quiet to reach an understanding of myself that was a foundation for being able to know yourself in the way that you have to know yourself to be an artist because you're different."

That legacy allowed her to communicate the "echoes" within herself through songwriting. "You can feel that echo multiplied a million times when you come to a place like this, and it's a huge, overwhelming, energizing place with so much opportunity to experience different kinds of music every night."

The Kentucky–New York creative axis that Joan describes naturally circles back to the question of home. She takes a long, contemplative sip of mint tea before responding. "This is going to sound really corny, but I feel like music is my home, and that's the place—whether I'm working with my band or writing something—where I feel like I'm in tune with what I need to be in tune with as this person who is living this life right now. It's not like I don't love the place—New York—that I have chosen as my physical home or I don't love to go home and be with my family in Kentucky and reconnect with that. But that feeling of aha, this is where I belong [is in my music]."

That emotion intensified in 2006 when Joan traveled to Nashville and fulfilled a lifelong dream by recording what she calls "my version of a country album," titled *Pretty Little Stranger.* Although initially nervous about how she would be received by the notoriously restrictive country music industry, she was overwhelmed by the amount of respect and acceptance she felt from the likes of Dolly Parton and Matraca Berg. Never one to follow a formula, Joan also insisted on pushing the boundaries, incorporating Middle Eastern musical elements and recording "After Jane," a song about a close relationship between two women that many read as a declaration of same-sex love. She also included new takes on material written by Rodney Crowell, Patty Griffin, Jerry Garcia, and Kris Kristofferson. "The vein that I was trying to tap into was more of like the late 1960s stuff, where rock 'n' roll and country really started to mix it up together," she says. "That was an exciting time, because that was a moment where country felt like, oh, we're going to step out and take a chance and do something different."

This willingness to challenge conventional wisdom is what ensures roots music's authenticity, Joan believes, a quality she continues to find revelatory and comforting. "There's something just so ultimately truthful about American roots music to me," she says, as a light breeze wafts through the restaurant's courtyard, rustling the thick ivy overhanging a portion of the fence. "It's kind of astonishing. When I'm writing a song, one of the things that I have is sort of a mantra: 'I need to tell the truth to myself before I can tell it to anyone else.'"

The grave expression on Joan's face underscores the sense of responsibility she feels to maintain this tradition of honesty. The arts, she believes—and music in particular—are becoming even more essential as an antidote to the increasing superficiality of contemporary culture. "We live in this society where it's about making enough money and getting to work and doing this appointment and achieving that goal. There are certain depths that we just sort of skirt around on a regular basis, and to me, that's what music can do for you, is just to wake up those parts of you that you've pushed aside because they're inconvenient and they get in the way of this streamlined, consuming, producing machine that we're all supposed to be now, living in this modern society."

Now an independent artist in an increasingly precarious industry, Joan is content with her status as a career singer-songwriter bursting with musical wanderlust. Her model, she reveals, has long been Tom Waits, a widely respected singer-songwriter with a faithful cult following. "He always put out interesting records," she says. "He could keep doing it without having the pressure of trying to be the big hot thing every minute. And strangely enough, I've kind of gotten around to that place after years and after that first tumultuous success."

Backstage at the famed Birchmere Music Hall in Alexandria, Virginia, Joan is sitting on a weathered leather loveseat in sweatpants and an oversized T-shirt. Guitar in hand, she is strumming lightly, singing to herself. As she bends closer to the guitar, intent on hearing a specific chord, locks of her tousled blonde hair lightly graze the lacquered body of the instrument.

Her road manager ushers in a local journalist for a brief introduction, breaking her concentration. If this irritates Joan, she gives no indication, graciously stopping in mid strum, leaning forward to grasp the reporter's hand, and exchanging a few pleasantries. "Thanks for coming," she says. "It's great to be back here. I've played here for years." As he exits, Joan hands off her guitar and wanders to her dressing room to prepare.

A mere thirty minutes later, her transformation is complete. She takes the stage in an electric blue minidress, her hazel eyes and pouty mouth framed by glossy curls. But instead of starting with a scorcher, she launches into a slow burn of a song from *Little Wild One* about her chosen hometown: "If I die in New York City / Bury me on the Battery."

Joan moves through her set list, a delicious cornucopia of roots genres, holding the sold-out room in the palm of her hand. They hang on every wail and inflection, mesmerized by her rich vibrato. She breaks into "Spider Web" from *Relish,* a gritty groove that she performs with her entire body, swaying back and forth, her hips moving in perfect rhythm, becoming the song. She brings her hand up to lightly graze the microphone—physical meeting spiritual. This is her native soil—Kentucky and New York combusting on the stage—her body and soul residing in the music.

As the show draws to a close, Joan pauses for a sip of water, and the guitarist breaks into that famous hook, the electric tremolo filling every corner of the room. There is no Nell Hampton tonight, only Joan, smiling from ear to ear, acknowledging the spontaneous applause of the audience, inviting them into her home for one more song.

Essential Tracks

"One of Us"
"Cathedrals"
"Pretty Little Stranger"
"On the Old Kentucky Shore" (with Ricky Skaggs)
"Light of This World"

7

Dwight Yoakam

A Hillbilly in Hollywood

They say our working and living environments are often windows into our psyches. If this is true, then Dwight Yoakam's office in the heart of Hollywood portrays a man at peace with his contradictions—loud yet refined, modern yet traditional, eclectic yet focused. Los Angeles meets Kentucky head-on.

There is a cow-print sofa—white with brown spots—and an antique barrister bookcase; a honeyed floor-model radio, circa 1935, and Herb Alpert's iconic *Whipped Cream* LP; a scattering of Andy Warhol art books and a handsome grandfather clock. Dozens of certificates stare down from the walls, records of Grammy nominations and awards, Recording Industry Association of America citations for gold and platinum albums, and a Screen Actors Guild nomination for Outstanding Performance by a Cast for his role in *Sling Blade*.

By the time he makes it to his office on Sunset Boulevard, Dwight is ready to put the cares of the day behind him. The appointment with his mechanic has taken longer than scheduled, forcing him to drive into Hollywood at the height of rush hour. He strides into the room in his boots—and his trademark painted-on jeans—full of apologies. And, proving that he has not left his

Dwight Yoakam: Los Angeles meets Kentucky head-on.
(Photo by Otto Felix)

hillbilly roots behind, his arms are loaded down with food for his guest—organic cherries and cashews.

He disappears after showing me into the conference room, an elongated space facing east that offers a stunning panorama of downtown Los Angeles up to the Hollywood Hills. Griffith Observatory, a Southern California landmark made famous by the classic film *Rebel Without a Cause,* is visible in the distance, its Art Deco copper domes and white-painted concrete walls luminous in the waning sunlight.

Dwight returns shortly with a bowl in each hand, the cherries freshly washed. We both dig in greedily, and soon we are down home, joking and quoting lines from *Coal Miner's Daughter,* the 1980 Academy Award–winning film about the life of beloved Kentuckian and country singer Loretta Lynn. He nearly doubles over as he describes the scene in which Loretta finds her husband, Doolittle, in the backseat of a car with another woman at a country fair.

> LORETTA: Woman, if you want to keep that arm you better get it off my husband.
> WOMAN: Who you tellin' what?
> LORETTA: I don't know who you are, but I know what you are.

I respond with another scene, when Loretta meets her idol Patsy Cline, who has been hospitalized after a serious car accident.

> LORETTA: I just can't believe I'm sittin' here talkin' to Patsy Cline.
> PATSY: You act like you ain't never seen a glamorous country music singer before.

As the laughter subsides, Dwight turns serious with one final reference. "'If you're born in Kentucky you got three choices: coal mine, moonshine, or move it on down the line.'" It's the perfect segue to his family's story, one that mirrors those of thousands of others from the mountains of Eastern Kentucky.

When Dwight was two, his parents, Ruth Ann and David, followed other family members from Floyd County in a migratory chain to Columbus, Ohio, in search of work, which his mother found as a keypunch operator at an automotive parts factory and his father by opening a gas station. Although Dwight was young enough to assimilate into this new culture, his parents were often the objects of scorn and discrimination, set apart by their mountain dialect and the traditions they maintained. "We ate squirrel," he laughs, "and nobody else in that zip code was firing up some squirrel too often."

Friday evenings, the family was so homesick for the kinfolk they had left behind in Store Holler, just outside Betsy Layne, that they would pile into the car and return, joining a caravan of countless other Appalachians making the journey down Route 23. "We were taillight babies," he says of himself and his younger brother and sister, "in that there were cars with Ohio and Michigan license plates that on Friday night streamed into southeastern Kentucky across the Ohio River at Portsmouth, Ironton, and all the way over into Cincinnati."

It was around 2:00 A.M. before he heard the crunch of dirt and gravel underneath the car's tires as it wound its way along the one-lane road to his maternal grandparents' home. Luther and Earlene Tibbs would still be up, the light from their windows a welcome sight for the weary children who tumbled out of the backseat into their arms. Saturdays were spent playing outside or traveling to nearby Pikeville, and after one such trip Dwight recalls returning home to find a robbery of sorts in progress. "Came back and my brother had locked my grandpa—" he stops in midsentence, howling with laughter, "in the washhouse and was making him slip quarters underneath [the door] to get out! My mother was outraged. My grandpa thought it was kind of funny."

The mood on Sunday morning before church was more somber, as the family knew their trek back to Ohio was looming. All through church and dinner afterward, that reality covered them like kudzu, taking over their thoughts and expressions. They said their good-byes in the late afternoon with long faces, as the family remaining behind in Kentucky attempted to bolster them: "You'll be back in five more days." And sure enough, they were, unwilling to forsake their Eastern Kentucky roots, unable to plant lasting ones in Ohio.

For children like Dwight, this foot-in-both-worlds approach shaped their lives. When he speaks now of his formative years, the majority of his stories take place in the car, traveling between Kentucky and Ohio. "Naomi Judd and I have laughed about gazing balls, which were mercury glass balls that were put in a birdbath base that you bought at the roadside stands all down through Route 23, all down along the way where the quilts were. You could buy a quilt and then buy a gazing ball."

The radio was a constant presence on these trips, he says, and they sang along to the current pop tunes as well as country songs by Hank Williams and Johnny Cash. During one of these long rides, Dwight had a vision of his future while listening to a country song. "I was in the backseat, and I remember listening and just watching those mountains and that world pass, and just having this epiphany that this was what I was going to be about outside of here. I didn't know what it meant, and I wasn't certain how this would come to fruition, but [I knew] for some reason I'm listening and driving and going in and out—back and forth—in this culture."

At 7021 Hollywood Boulevard, just over a mile from Dwight's office, lies a two-foot-square slab in the sidewalk bearing a pink five-pointed terrazzo star trimmed with brass and inlaid in a black-speckled stone background. The name DWIGHT YOA-KAM is spelled out in block letters in the upper half of the star, with a brass emblem of a phonograph inlaid below. Joining him on the Hollywood Walk of Fame are fellow Kentuckians the Everly

Brothers, whose star rests directly across the street. When his star was unveiled on 5 June 2003, Dwight addressed his mother from the microphone with an emotional understatement: "It's a long way from Pikeville, Kentucky, huh?"

Dwight Yoakam as an Actor

For Dwight, acting has never been a side venture. At Northland High School in Columbus, Ohio, he appeared in productions of *The Miracle Worker, Flowers for Algernon,* and assorted variety shows. Years later, he brought his acting skills to music videos, including one for "Honky Tonk Man," the first country music video to be played on MTV. But it wasn't until 1991 that he made his big-screen debut with a bit part in *Terminator 2: Judgment Day.*

By 1996, he had graduated from small roles to more meaty material, turning in an iconic performance as the raging alcoholic Doyle Hargraves in *Sling Blade,* opposite Billy Bob Thornton. Since then, he has starred alongside Hollywood heavyweights Jodie Foster (*Panic Room*), Tommy Lee Jones (*The Three Burials of Melquiades Estrada*), and Reese Witherspoon (*Four Christmases*), showing off expansive dramatic and comedic ranges. With the release of *South of Heaven, West of Hell* in 2000, Dwight added director and screenwriter to his résumé.

Dwight laughs as he remembers an exchange with Tommy Lee Jones during the making of *The Three Burials of Melquiades Estrada.* The film, set in west Texas and Mexico, was being directed by Jones—himself no stranger to Kentucky, having starred as Doolittle Lynn opposite Sissy Spacek's Loretta in *Coal Miner's Daughter.* One night on the looping stage, Dwight couldn't quite shake his Kentucky roots. "'Dwight,' [Jones said], 'you need to loop that line again.' I said, 'I thought it looked like I was in sync really well.' He said, 'Oh no, it was in sync. It just had too much Ohio River and not enough Pecos.'"

Two thousand miles from Route 23, Dwight has built a decades-long career in both music and film, experiencing widespread commercial success without sacrificing an ounce of artistic integrity. With twenty-five million albums sold worldwide, twelve gold records and nine platinum or multiplatinum records, and two Grammy Awards to his credit, he is one of country music's most successful artists. He has also proved to be one hell of an actor, racking up critically acclaimed performances in a wide range of movies, including *Sling Blade, Panic Room,* and *Wedding Crashers.*

Night falls over the city as we continue to talk in the conference room. Up in the hills, columns of floodlights illuminate Griffith Observatory, and my mind wanders again to its famed link to *Rebel Without a Cause.* That word—*rebel*—hangs in the air, lurking underneath the long table and behind the door, alluded to but never spoken. Not that it has to be, for in many ways, Dwight is the quintessential country music rebel, demanding a career in that famously conservative industry on his own terms. It's worth noting that after a brief, unfulfilling stint in Nashville, he sought the more open and experimental music scene of Los Angeles in 1977.

"There wasn't a country music community here," he recalls, "which was good for me because I was able to move among the rock community, and there was a cow-punk movement that started. There's always been—since the Steinbeck kind of *Grapes of Wrath,* Okie-Arkie Dust Bowl migration out here—a legacy of country music in LA."

In seeking to make his mark as a musical transplant, Dwight closely studied the area's cultural history. He points east out the window and describes at length how the cross streets of Sunset Boulevard and Gower Avenue took on the moniker Gower Gulch during the 1930s: that was where the cowboy actors would congregate in full garb, hoping to get work as extras in the westerns made at the nearby movie studios. This migratory culture, he says, gave birth to bands like the Byrds, who were pioneers in combining country and rock music, and he connects that legacy to his own. "There's a culture of transplants, or of being from the outside, that's part of California that probably allowed me to really tap into the experiences that my family had going to Ohio or to Detroit."

He began to connect to that culture (in between hours spent working on a department store loading dock) by driving to the Palomino Club in North Hollywood—dubbed "country music's most important West Coast club" by the *Los Angeles Times*—and catching shows by artists including Linda Ronstadt, Merle Haggard, and future mentor Buck Owens. And his youthful premonition slowly revealed itself as he began mining his family's history and Eastern Kentucky roots in his songwriting.

When his beloved grandfather Luther Tibbs died, Dwight coped with the loss by further immersing himself in his art, penning two songs that would be pivotal cuts on future records. "Miner's Prayer" is a sobering account of Tibbs's forty-year tenure as an underground coal miner, opening with a plea to Christ to "please let me see the sunshine one more time." But "Floyd County" goes one step further, taking the listener to his grandpa's grave on a hillside back in Eastern Kentucky. The brilliance of the song lies in its specific details, images of grief so vivid that they instantly become universal. He portrays Tibbs as a "soft-spoken mountain man" who provided for his six children "with the money / he earned in those black mines / and the food he could raise with his hands."

The subject of his grandparents is an emotional one for Dwight, and he instinctually turns to glance out the window toward the brown-sculpted hills, so different in topography from his native Kentucky. The comparison must be on his mind as well,

"My music . . . is an expression of the love I felt and the familial culture that I knew." —Dwight Yoakam (Photo courtesy of artist's management)

because when he looks back around, he recalls his mother's first visit to a house he was renting in the Hollywood Hills. "I got up [there] and drove her around. She said, 'Lord have mercy, it's just like a holler! Look at that house up there on the stilts! It's an expensive holler!'"

His change of subject is not a diversion, however, just an unfiltered stream of consciousness that soon returns to the matter at hand. "What I was able to do, hopefully—and I say this with a strong, profound sense of emotional obligation to my grandparents . . . ," he tears up and trails off. "My music, I hope, is an expression of the love I felt and the familial culture that I knew. I think had I not moved so far away, things wouldn't have crystallized so acutely for me as a writer perhaps. I was certainly able from this vantage point to write in a more specific way because I only had my thoughts to recall everything by. So I had to pull elements that were tactile—you know, the shale rock. When we crossed over that river and got down in there, that's when you knew [you were back home]. You saw it along the river on the other side, but not like when you crossed over at Ashland."

By the time he got around to recording demos of these and other songs in 1981, the landscape of country music was changing significantly. The release of *Urban Cowboy* the year before had sparked a nationwide spike in Bud and Sissy wannabes (the film's main characters, portrayed by John Travolta and Debra Winger), ushering in a more modern, pop-oriented brand of country music. With his self-described "electrified bluegrass" sound, Dwight's music ran counter to this trend, hearkening back to the rockabilly music of the 1950s. But the California cow-punk scene was kind, and he spent the next few years playing rough and rowdy bars and developing his own style, a melding of Floyd County and the Bakersfield sound popularized by Buck Owens and Merle Haggard. His distinct voice, with its high, piercing tones, came straight out of the mouth of Store Holler. When legendary West Coast disc jockey Joe Nixon heard him croon "Please Daddy" on those early demos, he turned to Dwight's producer and remarked, "You can hear that Kentucky in him. Listen to when he sings the word *Daddy*."

As Dwight built a name for himself on the LA music scene, he became confident enough to release an indie EP in 1984 titled *Guitars, Cadillacs, Etc., Etc.*, which generated big buzz and was widely played on college radio. By this time, neotraditional artists such as Keith Whitley, the Judds, and Ricky Skaggs had arrived on the scene and were beginning to rein in some of pop country's most flagrant excesses (cue "Through the Years" by Kenny Rogers). Less than a year later, Warner Bros. Records was knocking on his door, offering Dwight a record deal and agreeing to expand the EP by four songs. One of those was a cover of an old Johnny Horton song, "Honky Tonk Man." After its release in early 1986, the single remained on the country charts for six months, peaking at number three. Its B-side was "Miner's Prayer."

Guitars, Cadillacs, Etc., Etc. was met with rave reviews, making Dwight a member of the so-called Class of '86, a year that featured debuts by fellow neotraditionalists Randy Travis, Steve Earle, and Lyle Lovett. "It was bittersweet," Yoakam says of the acclaim. "I mean, it was certainly a vindication of things I'd felt personally along the way, because it was nine years into being out here. In quiet moments alone I was melancholy that Earlene and Luther Tibbs, the two people who most profoundly affected that part of my musical life, didn't get to see it come to fruition."

Even in death, his grandparents continued to provide inspiration for his music, he says, pointing to an original song on his debut album titled "South of Cincinnati." A wistful ballad about leaving Kentucky to find work in a factory in Ohio, the song was not a strict biography of his grandparents—they never left the mountains. But it was full of their spirit, he says. "The two of them were profoundly connected to my being. They were the embodiment, in my mind's eye, for the stoicism that's in that song—my grandfather's quiet resolve, my grandmother's visible stoicism and her strength. There's something about the mountain culture that I maybe had the benefit of being removed from, so I had a graphic focus on it."

In many ways, "South of Cincinnati" can be seen as a warm-up exercise for a song on Dwight's next record, the aptly titled *Hillbilly Deluxe*. Released in 1987, it shot to number one on the country charts, muscled by the singles "Little Ways," "Please, Please Baby," and a sex-and-gasoline cover of Elvis Presley's "Little Sister." But "Readin', Rightin', Rt. 23" was in many ways the album's centerpiece, rooted in his childhood spent in the backseat of the family car as it shuttled them between Floyd County and Columbus.

"They didn't know that old highway / could lead them to a world of misery," he sings, recalling those late nights when they would "pull up in a holler about 2 A.M. and see a light still shining bright" from his grandparents' home. The genesis of the song came from an exchange the young Dwight had with a member of his parents' church in Columbus. "He said, 'Well, you know what they say that the three R's they teach in Kentucky schools are, Dwight—readin' and writin' and Route 23 North.'" He pauses to collect a handful of cashews. "I wrote the song about that experience, about my mother's generation suffering the belittlement, culturally, of folks that are part of Appalachia, too, by the way, in Ohio—they just don't know it! [We] at the time were the brunt of that joke. And then hopefully I was able to turn the joke inside out."

Dwight tells a story about recording a song with Dr. Ralph Stanley for his 1997 album *Under the Covers*. He had recruited the bluegrass icon to play banjo on a cover of the Clash's classic punk song "Train in Vain," and after Stanley had laid down a track, he ambled into the control booth. "He came back in to listen, and the engineer [nodding toward a banjo] looked at him and said, 'Well, that's a seven chord there, Ralph. Do you want to play the seven?' And Ralph stood there and kind of rocked back and forth. He said, 'No sir, hit ain't the mountain way.'" A great big belly laugh rolls out of Dwight and bounces off the windows. "So we just left that chord alone!"

An offhand response in the studio, Stanley's comment is nonetheless a fitting summary of Appalachian culture—fiercely independent, a bit cantankerous, weighing one's options and choosing the path of integrity. It is a lesson Dwight learned at the feet of Luther and Earlene Tibbs and in the backseat of the family car, absorbing the sights and sounds of his native region.

"It was just there by osmosis," he explains. "I didn't have to be taught about mountain music. All I had to do was listen to them sing in the car. All you had to do was turn that radio on. We were *doing* mountain music up and down the road."

He hopes to pass on this spirit of creative independence and fidelity to one's native culture to young artists in the region. Along with E. Keith Stotts, an old friend from Columbus who is now president of Ohio Valley University in Vienna, West Virginia, Dwight hopes to found an Appalachian Center on the college's campus and create an outreach program for youth. Their vision, he says, is to encourage artistically minded students to "reach outside their cloistered world and aspire to perhaps go outside the culture at some point in their life and bring back those experiences to their own homes." A key component, Dwight explains, will be awarding scholarships to students from the region, with the requirement that they return every summer to tutor and teach college preparatory classes to high school students, "to be a touchstone." They even have a name for the program: Traveler's Lanterns, taken from a song on his record *A Long Way Home.*

> Won't you set out a traveler's lantern
> Just a small light that they might see
> To guide them back home

Like so much of his creative work, this endeavor reflects the presence of his grandparents. Perhaps he returned to the long car rides of his youth when he wrote "Traveler's Lantern," recalling a light shining from the windows of an old coal camp house in Store Holler in the dark of night. That beacon has become a metaphor, the inheritance of Luther and Earlene Tibbs, passed on to their grandson, who continues to honor them in his music. Their legacy of stoicism and fierce independence continues to define his career choices.

"It has to feel natural to me. I've always reacted negatively to anything and withdrew from anything that didn't feel honest and earnest. Maybe it's like Ralph Stanley, that night the engineer asked him to play the seven chord. 'Hit ain't the mountain way.'"

Essential Tracks

"Bury Me" (with Maria McKee)
"Floyd County"
"Readin', Rightin', Rt. 23"
"Send a Message to My Heart" (with Patty Loveless)
"I Sang Dixie"

8

Nappy Roots

The Pursuit of Nappyness

The Louisville skyline is a welcome sight on a summer evening. With only a dozen or so skyscrapers, the city does not convey an overwhelming presence. To the contrary, the buildings are a comfort, almost like a small chain of mountains that are both welcoming and mysterious. The Romanesque dome of the Aegon Center is the focal point, its peak illuminated from within at night by a series of muted lights. Viewed from across the river in Indiana, even the John F. Kennedy Memorial Bridge, which carries I-65 across the muddy Ohio River, appears to blend in with the urban landscape.

This panorama has been the subject of hundreds of photographs taken from the popular *Belle of Louisville*, a steamboat constructed in 1914 that offers public excursions and dinner cruises. But it had likely not been featured on an album cover until 2010, when the southern rap group Nappy Roots released its fourth album, *The Pursuit of Nappyness*. The artwork paid tribute to the hometown of Nappy Roots front man Skinny Deville and fellow group members Clutch and B-Stille—a striking sepia-toned rendering of the Louisville skyline resting under an image of a tree with its roots extended downward toward the city.

Nappy Roots has become known for combining images of rural Kentucky with thumping urban beats, so this tribute to the members' hometown was hardly a surprise. One of the tracks, though, was more poignant than usual, a gentle rap laid down over an acoustic guitar, Dobro, and ever-present bass line: "Life's good but it definitely ain't easy / Remember we was kids, just nappy-headed, greasy." And then the chorus, a feel-good sing-along packed full of truth:

> We can make it on our own
> But we ain't got to be alone
> Just in case when things go wrong
> You can always come back home

Dubbed "recession rap" by music critics, for its emphasis on staying positive during hard times, *The Pursuit of Nappyness* was the group's second independent release, coming on the heels of a wildly successful but volatile stint with powerhouse Atlantic Records, where Nappy Roots sold 1.5 million copies of its debut album. The title, a play on the blockbuster movie *The Pursuit of Happyness* starring Will Smith, also referred to their hard-won artistic freedom, says Skinny—music made on their own terms.

"Like Will Smith—[the character he played] was losing his ass with everything, he was losing his family, and he did what he had to do to survive and take care of his family and his son. He sacrificed and sacrificed and sacrificed just to be able to take care of his son. And so to me, that movie symbolized a lot of things that were going on in a lot of people's lives. We say, 'How far are you going to go to keep it real?' It's the pursuit—everybody's always on the chase for the next big thing, and for Nappy Roots that was making music. And that's exactly what we did—we took a pay cut, we got back on the road. We made music again that didn't try to be like anybody else, and the songs on that album represent us staying true to what we do."

Skinny Deville and Scales of Nappy Roots. (Photo courtesy of artists' management)

What Nappy Roots does is roots rap—a gritty blend of dusty guitars, catchy pop hooks, high-octane beats, and clever rhymes that celebrate where the group is from. This, Skinny says, was the intention from the beginning. "I always believed one person could make Kentucky rap. Nobody ever had. We wanted people to know that folks from Kentucky have talent to be reckoned with."

William Rahsaan Hughes, aka Skinny Deville, arrived on the campus of Western Kentucky University in Bowling Green in the fall of 1993, eager to escape the strict gaze of his parents back in Jeffersontown, a suburb of Louisville. Although excited to be on his own, he admits that he was also glad to get away from the dangerous culture plaguing his hometown.

"There was a lot of violence in Louisville at the time. Someone was dying like on a daily or weekly basis. And it was just better for me to disassociate myself from my old set of friends and hang out with some people who actually wanted to do some things more productive in life."

One of his new friends was Ronald Wilson, a tall, skinny guy from Louisville who soon became known as Ron Clutch. The two bonded over similar values and beliefs, as well as a love for hip-hop. Like most college students, Skinny and Clutch also shared a love of partying and eventually moved off campus with two other guys to a house on Kentucky Avenue that shared a parking lot with a large church. "Our house was like the party house for everybody," Skinny laughs. "We'd use the parking lot to park all the cars, and everything you can think of went down in this house. It probably wasn't, you know, religious."

The soundtrack for their epic house parties was made up of southern hip-hop, a new flavor of the genre that was based in Atlanta and put on the map by OutKast and Goodie Mob, an influential group that included Cee Lo Green. Skinny and Clutch inhaled hits like Goodie Mob's "Cell Therapy" and OutKast's "Player's Ball" as eagerly as they did their ever-present doobies, and before long, they hit upon an idea.

"We'd smoke weed before we'd get to class every day," Skinny says. "I was smoking and thinking and shit, brainstorming, and brain fart every thirty seconds. It was stupid high ideas. So one day me and Clutch are walking to class, and he says we should start a rap group. And it hit me: Damn, I'd been writing raps for a while, but nobody knew about it. But you know what—if they could do it, we could do it. [Clutch] was playing; I was serious about it. It was a no-brainer. He would come back after class and play video games. I went to the bookstore and bought a notebook and three great pens and started writing like I used to, back in third and eighth and freshman year [of high school]. It was like a light switch. It was like an epiphany."

Skinny became consumed with the prospect, writing down everything and constantly rapping around the house in between classes and working "more bad jobs than you can get." At one point, after going three weeks without a haircut, his hair began to kink, and he stumbled on the group's name. "I'm rapping, 'My roots are so nappy / I'm still happy,' some shit like that, and I'd put in another verse. Clutch [would] put in a verse about my nappy roots, and just like that we started saying *Nappy Roots*."

Soon afterward, the pair added to their ranks Vito Jermaine Tisdale, a hulking boy from Bowling Green who became known as Big V; fellow Louisville native Brian Scott, who took the name B-Stille; Melvin Adams Jr., a college basketball player from Milledgeville, Georgia, now known as Fish Scales; and Ryan Anthony from Oakland, California, who evolved into R. Prophet.

After recording a song at the house, the new group set out to make an entire album. When they learned that two of their friends were planning to open a record store in Bowling Green, the guys proposed dividing the space—the store on one side, and a recording studio on the other—and splitting the rent. "I had a little bit of money," Skinny recalls. "We talked to people and got some investments, got some equipment. Sold my car, a Jetta—I was doing whatever for my career. I'm like, I'll walk to school. Fuck it. We made up T-shirts; they sold like hotcakes. We sold to sororities and fraternities. We'd make up shirts that were the color of their fraternities instead of just black and white. Everybody was loving Nappy Roots."

Country Fried Cess was released independently in 1998, and Skinny and company worked nearly around the clock to spread the word about it. An edgy record about Louisville, it resonated with college kids at Western Kentucky University and back home, generating massive buzz in the region—and beyond, it turned out. Before the year ended, Atlantic Records had come calling. "It sold so good they heard about it," Skinny hoots now. After signing a contract, Nappy Roots was back in the studio, working on a major label debut.

"We pretty much developed our sound. [Atlantic] said, 'You gonna play this country shit even though you from Louisville and ain't that country.'" The idea didn't set well with Skinny at first, but he soon saw the genius of it. "People from Louisville don't consider themselves country, but if you go outside Kentucky, people think you country. They said, 'Just play into it—you're from Kentucky, so play it up,' and that's what got us off the shelf."

Skinny Deville On . . .

His early musical influences: "Stevie Wonder. I really like Stevie Wonder. Like 'Hotter than July' and 'Master Blaster,' you know. He's one of my inspirations, other than my parents. This guy did it blind. This guy was a musical genius, and he transcended his culture and his times to be an impact on everybody else's culture and time."

The heritage of black musicians from Kentucky: "Those people before us did things that got us where we are. There's a lot of people that come out of Kentucky. We want to keep the torch burning, not just through Nappy Roots but also through tax dollars—keeping the orchestra and choirs and band going on in school."

His home state: "What I love about Kentucky is that I can close my eyes, and I can imagine myself coming home from school in the fall, and I can see all those leaves changing color . . . from green to yellow and orange and red. That's the most beautiful thing. How green our grass is. Who the people are. Whether you white or black. Bowling Green supported us. Louisville supported us. Kentucky supported us."

When *Watermelon, Chicken & Gritz* debuted in February 2002, music critics treated its country-tinged rap as a breath of fresh air. "Their down-home guitar plucks, easy-going flows and comical lyrics are some of the only things we have right now to counter all of the Courvoisier-sippin' and Escalade-drivin' mainstream hip hop has to offer," wrote *Hip Hop DX* with a nearly audible sigh of relief. The album's first single, a catchy, hook-laden track called "Awnaw," gave a forceful shout-out to their home state:

> My yegga, we hogwild, bet that from that roota to that
>> toota-file
> Hell naw, them country boys ain't headed south for six miles
> Kentucky mud, them kinfolk, twankies with them
>> hundred-spokes
> Skullied on that front porch, plus you know they got 'dro

The song swiftly rose to number eighteen on the *Billboard* Hot R&B/Hip-Hop chart and reached number fifty-one on the Hot 100. But the single's success was overshadowed by its follow-up, "Po' Folks," a rootsy, working-class rap about "front porch, chillin' broke, country folk" with an irresistible beat that features southern soul crooner Anthony Hamilton on the chorus:

> All my life been po'
> But it really don't matter no mo'
> And they wonder why we act this way
> Nappy Boys gonna be okay

The song became a sensation, entering the top ten on the *Billboard* Hot Rap chart and vaulting to number twenty-one on the Hot 100. When the Grammy Award nominees were announced later that year, "Po' Folks" received a nod for Best Rap/Sung Collaboration (the prize ultimately went to "Dilemma" by Nelly and

Kelly Rowland). *Watermelon, Chicken & Gritz* was on its way to achieving platinum status.

Besides the group's embrace of rural life, Nappy Roots attracted attention for its refusal to objectify women and glorify violence in its music, consciously choosing to promote a positive message instead—a quality that Skinny continues to speak of with great pride. He grows distressed when I mention that transcribed lyrics to their song "Blowin' Trees" are making the rounds on the Internet and include a homophobic reference. "No, no, no. We would never do that. Never, never. We at Nappy Roots are not homophobic. We have friends who are homosexual." That discrepancy, he says, simply does not fit into the progressive Nappy Roots philosophy, which he describes as personally "very important."

"I always liked songs that had something more to them outside the beat. My point from day one, the guys will tell you, was after the beat stops, what's going to keep people liking you? You have to say something. Hip-hop now is so pointless sometimes. I'm older now, but what I'm experiencing, what I'm liking, is different from those teenagers who don't know about paying bills and having to pay taxes and raising kids. It's very different. For me, I've always wanted to have a message and a point and a moral. That's what's gotten us to where we are right now because it's more than the beat. It's cooler than just the beat. It's cooler than just the hook. Listen to the verses. Listen to what we're saying.

"If I talk about how much ice I have and how much my Gucci flats and the Maserati [cost]—there ain't even no Maserati dealership in Louisville! There is no Louis Vuitton store in Bowling Green. I can't talk about those things I never experienced. I have to talk about what I know. I ain't no gangster. I didn't grow up killin'. I grew up with both my parents in a middle-class neighborhood. Both my parents worked. They knew the value of a dollar. At the time we came out, Master P was going on about cash money and the word *bling-bling* hadn't even came out. I'm like, 'Shit, you got a helicopter? This cat got a solid gold Porsche?' I can't say that. I'm a guy at Western trying to rap, and everybody knew these guys were full of shit, and they looked at Nappy Roots and they'd say, 'Man, keep it real.' I had earned their trust. We trained ourselves early on to say something. Our music definitely has a point."

The widespread success of *Watermelon, Chicken & Gritz* guaranteed that Nappy Roots would receive accolades from nearly every corner. One of the most meaningful plaudits came close to home when Governor Paul Patton declared 16 September 2002 "Nappy Roots Day" throughout the commonwealth of Kentucky. To Skinny, that honor represents why the state occupies such a singular place in his soul.

"I've rapped around Jewish people, crackers, people who lived in the hood, white people, black people. None of that matters in the nitty-gritty of Kentucky, and everybody from Kentucky loves everybody because we're from Kentucky. We can put racial or financial stipulations on it, but deep down, it's about being from Kentucky. You see somebody broke down on the side of the road, you stop and help them no matter what color they are. I'll always have a love for Kentucky."

Skinny's commitment to the state continued with the group's follow-up *Wooden Leather*, released in late 2003 and featuring assists from Kanye West, Raphael Saadiq, and Lil John, along with repeat performances by Anthony Hamilton. "The whole damn world's country," they proclaimed on "Roun' the Globe," the album's lead single: "Been all around the globe from Monday to Sunday / Y'all the same folk we see in Kentucky." The infectious groove peaked at number twenty-five on the Hot Rap Tracks chart, driving *Wooden Leather* to number twelve on the Hot 100 Albums.

Though not the smash that *Watermelon, Chicken & Gritz* was, the record continued to expand Nappy Roots' fan base, serving up energetic beats and quick rhymes. R. Prophet exited the group following the release of *Wooden Leather* to pursue a solo career, and Atlantic Records began leaning on the guys to scale back even further. "They wanted to make the group smaller to be more cost-effective," Skinny explains. "And you know, before I let any kind of industry anything split up a bunch of guys that are brothers for the sake of money—like I'm not going to do that. If we're going to fall out, it's because we're too old and don't want it no more. That's what's going to end Nappy Roots. Old age. It's not going to be about money."

In the wake of the unprecedented success of the Black Eyed Peas, a hip-hop act that had recently added Stacy Ferguson (Fergie) to its lineup, Skinny says the record label wanted to try something similar with Nappy Roots to "make them more marketable." They refused, discussing their options before deciding to part ways with Atlantic. "It was Scales's idea that we should go independent. We already got the brains, we're already famous and shit. We sold a million records, and we really didn't make any money. They said we owed it all to them."

He says the group had to "play dead" for two years to secure a release from its contract in 2007, but the liberation was worth the wait. They released *The Humdinger* the following year; it was newly founded Nappy Roots Entertainment Group's first album. *The Humdinger* continued the group's chart success, peaking at number seven on the *Billboard* Rap Albums chart and receiving rave reviews from *DJ Booth* and *Hip Hop DX*.

After touring extensively, the guys returned to the studio to record *The Pursuit of Nappyness,* which debuted in mid-2010 with its message of perseverance in trying economic times. "It is recession rap," Skinny admits. "We talk about where we was trying to go, and when you sing like morals and certain words, I mean, it's okay to be where you at. 'I'm gonna be alright. I'm gonna be okay. Long as I got you we gonna find a way.' You know?"

Skinny is on his way to the studio in Atlanta, zipping through the city's notorious traffic to meet up with Nappy Roots' producers. After all these years, the group finally has the opportunity to work with Organized Noise, the producers of OutKast and Goodie Mob, the southern hip-hop acts that had such an influence on Skinny and Clutch during their college years back in Bowling Green.

Scheduled for release in late September 2011, *Nappy Dot Org* promises to be "phenomenal," Skinny says excitedly, already trying out his media pitch. "What you're going to get is a crazy album. The beats are crazy, the concepts are still likeminded and Nappy Roots thought processes, but we're just turning it up a thousand degrees. [Our producers are] just reshaping and redefining what we've always done and making it better than what it always has been. I'm excited."

Despite the ups and downs of the music industry over the last decade, Skinny says that he can't imagine doing anything else. He realizes that Nappy Roots is fortunate to still be on the scene after fifteen years, especially considering that "hip-hop has a very short life span." He's more reflective these days, at a point in his career where he's pondering the influences on his music. Kentucky, he says, is at the top of the list.

"We are in the middle of a lot of things. It's a couple of hours from Chicago. It's a couple of hours from Nashville, so the country scene bleeds up. The Midwest bleeds down. The East Coast hip-hop comes over. The West Coast love comes in. If you look at Kentucky, we're like the hub of a wheel. We're not so far down south that we don't hear what's going on up north. And we're not so far up north that we don't recognize what's going on down south, even with Memphis and the blues. Look at jazz. Look at country. It's all right there."

Essential Tracks

"Po' Folks"
"Roun' the Globe"
"Country Boyz"
"Come Back Home"
"Awnaw"

9

Matraca Berg

Headwaters

The headwaters of the Cumberland River are pristine. Like many residents of Eastern Kentucky, they have carved out a path over time, trickling down from the surrounding mountaintops and into the hollers below. Each of the three tributaries—Poor Fork, Clover Fork, Martins Fork—flows briskly through Harlan County over beds of rock, past the small communities along their banks. Sand Hill, Ages, Grays Knob. They meander into the town of Baxter like three unruly tree branches, joining at the confluence to form the trunk of the river itself. Its current winds lazily toward Pineville alongside U.S. Highway 119, drifting under swinging bridges and modern concrete and steel overpasses.

Like most other geographic boundaries, the Cumberland River marks the lives of the people who live on its banks. This is especially true in Wallins Creek—just a few miles from the Bell County line—where one of the town's communities is called "Across the River." Founded in the late 1800s, Wallins Creek quickly became a booming mining town. By 1912, the hamlet boasted three hotels, two theaters, a bank, several restaurants, an A&P grocery store, two pool halls and bars, a candy kitchen, and various other businesses, all connected by an elaborate board-walk. Despite the town's steady growth, much of its wealth was shipped out on railroad cars, carried north through the Cumberland Mountains and Ohio River Valley to Dearborn, Michigan. There, Wallins Creek coal helped build Henry Ford's automotive empire.

After a fire destroyed the burgeoning town in the early 1920s, its residents were determined to rebuild. Their efforts were so successful that Royal Crown Cola erected a bottling plant there. A big band entertained the locals in one of the bars. But as Wallins Creek's mines began to close in midcentury, many businesses also shut their doors. Countless families joined the Great Appalachian Migration, moving north in search of factory jobs at companies like Mosler in Cincinnati and General Motors in Detroit.

The Cumberland River remained a constant throughout this upheaval, a physical and spiritual marker for the people who remained in Wallins Creek.

They knew that to be fully "washed in the blood of the Lamb," they first had to be cleansed in the murky waters of the Cumberland. Congregations speckled its banks on Sundays during warm weather, murmuring a ragged chorus of "Bless her, Lord" and "Thank you, Jesus" that impelled the new believer to join the preacher out in the current.

Total immersion, this was, and she became one with the river, plunging beneath its surface, her dress ballooning in a pocket of air.

"Hallelujah," shouted the observers along the riverbank, knowing that they, too, had been baptized in its flow, marked by the inevitable April floods, the bluegill on their supper tables, the swimming hole of their youth.

The Cumberland was part of their collective memory, a current connecting them to their sons and daughters and grandchildren who had crossed its border in search of better opportunities. They knew that to leave these waters was to never truly be gone.

Matraca Berg left Wallins Creek in utero, carried away from the place of her conception by a Greyhound bound for Nashville. As the bus sped around the treacherous curves of Highway 119, Icie Calloway's desperation must have been palpable.

Perhaps she stared vacantly out the window at the passing cliff faces, numb after being abandoned by the baby's father. Or maybe she simply smoothed her cotton dress and let out a weary sigh, punctuating the longing she felt for a stable life and career as a singer-songwriter in the capital of country music. Regardless, the eighteen-year-old Icie had few choices in 1964, an era in which unwed girls "in trouble" were sent away before their indiscretions began to show.

"She had to get out of Wallins to keep up appearances," Matraca explains, "so she came here to have me."

Forty-six years later, Matraca is perched in a booth at Fido, a hip coffee shop located in Nashville's Hillsboro Village. It's a surprisingly warm afternoon in early March, and the doors of Fido are wide open, allowing the sounds of pedestrians and traffic to trickle in from Twenty-first Avenue. They mingle with the shouts of two baristas straining to be heard over the roar of a blender and espresso machine.

Matraca tests her chamomile tea in silence. Bitter. She stirs in a few drops of honey. Another sip. Just right. She returns the fat cup to the table two-handed.

Her angular features look flawless against the lacquered wood of the bench, framed by strands of mocha-colored hair that cascade down past her shoulders. But the focal point of her face is a pair of dark, wide-set eyes that say everything. They are equal parts power and vulnerability, joy and melancholy, a rich brew that reveals a mature knowledge of the world and its workings. One glance conveys that she knows what it means to be an outsider, to defy the odds. Make no mistake: Matraca Berg is fierce.

"I was born in Vanderbilt Hospital, right down the street there," she nods. "She put me up for adoption. And I guess there was a grace period, and she changed her mind and got me back."

Icie and her newborn daughter with the "exotic hillbilly" name settled with her sister Sudie—a noted background singer for George Jones, Curtis Young, and Rita Figlio—and brother-in-law Jim Baker, who later played steel guitar for Mel Tillis. "She didn't want to go back to Wallins with a baby, so she was kind of stuck here," Matraca says.

Icie still dreamed of a career in the country music industry, especially after witnessing the success of Sudie, who had also performed for years with sisters Clara and Coleida as the Calloway Sisters on the Renfro Valley Barn Dance. But while staying with cousins in Oak Ridge, Icie met Ron Berg, a physicist who was conducting research at the Oak Ridge National Laboratory. Ron was the son of a dairy farmer in rural Wisconsin, and Matraca speculates that he and Icie bonded over their country roots: "Rural and bright—maybe that's what connected them."

They married and settled in Nashville, where Ron was in graduate school at Vanderbilt University. He adopted Matraca, and Icie took on the role of homemaker. It was a demanding task, caring for a new family while still nursing her own personal ambitions. Perhaps it was inevitable that her yearning to be a songwriter was absorbed by the young Matraca. After all, those longings had been incubating in Icie's body along with her daughter, and she clung to them just as she had ultimately chosen to keep her child.

Now, Matraca cups her slender hands around her tea, wondering aloud if her own birth might have prevented the emergence of her mother's musical aspirations.

"I think there was always circumstances or people holding Mom in her place. And me," she whispers. "It was just sad, really. After she married my dad and got pregnant again, it was just harder and harder for her. You need a lot of freedom when you're young and you're trying to go in."

This spiritual transference from mother to daughter led Matraca to write her first song at the age of five. "My dad used to carry me around Vanderbilt when nobody could watch me," she says. "I would go sit in a corner and color while he was working on research. I was making up a song, and he had those big computer board sheets they used to have back then. And he wrote down the song on the sheet and showed it to my mom."

Because both of Matraca's siblings were younger—her sister by four years and her brother by eight—she learned to entertain herself, becoming comfortable with and comforted by solitude. "I was kind of a loner," she says. "I wasn't screaming on a playground with a bunch of kids. I just never was that kid."

Instead, she spent her free time in front of her parents' record player, engrossed in an album collection that included artists from a variety of musical genres: Mickey Newbury, the Beatles, Herb Alpert and the Tijuana Brass, Lois Johnson, Don Gibson. But it was a woman from Chickasaw County, Mississippi, who really caught Matraca's eye and ear. "I worshipped Bobbie Gentry," she says. "She was so beautiful. I was obsessed with her and Dolly Parton because they played guitar and wrote their own songs and looked good."

Matraca also drew inspiration from her Kentucky roots. Icie made Wallins Creek a presence in their Nashville home, telling stories about her own childhood along the Cumberland River. "My mother and her siblings had such a love for growing up there. She talked about the coal companies and how everything was run

"When your family has been in a region for hundreds of years, you can't help but feel some kind of connectedness." —Matraca Berg (Photo by Glen Rose)

back in the day. The company store, the kind of community it was and how—when it was done—it all kind of dried up."

Eventually, enough time passed that Icie felt comfortable returning to Wallins Creek with her family, driving back to Kentucky over the same highways that had taken her to her exile in Nashville just a few years before. These monthlong visits provided Matraca with a physical landscape to complement the cultural geography she had come to know from her mother's stories.

"We went up there all the time," she recalls. "Every summer. We loved going up there. Mining was gone by the time we were kids, but you could still see the tipple and the kudzu growing up over it. We'd run like wild Indians and dam up the creeks and run up the hillsides."

Matraca felt an instant kinship to her rural playground. "We were city kids, so it was like paradise back then. When your family has been in a region for hundreds of years, you can't help but feel some kind of connectedness. That's just one place where I know I belong."

She underscores this point by ticking off the surnames of her southeastern Kentucky blood kin: Calloway, Hensley, Howard, Asher, Saylor. These are some of the oldest families in Harlan and Bell counties, a fact that Matraca acknowledges. "We were the first settlers to come over the Cumberland Gap."

They became farmers and miners, she says, giving a condensed family history that could belong to anyone in the mountains. Like most Appalachians, Matraca marks her family's history by place, breaking up her relatives' lives in sections according to where they lived: Her grandmother was born in Rose Hill, Virginia, and moved over the mountain to Harlan as a child. Her grandfather grew up in Bell County and went to work for his uncle's Creech Mining Company right out of school. His brother Boone followed him but was killed in a bulldozing accident at a young age. Her grandparents married and settled in Wallins Creek.

"In Wallins, I'm related to every other person, it seems. Part of it," she says, "is just having such a large family."

Matraca Berg as a Songwriter

Number-One Hits

"Faking Love"	T. G. Sheppard and Karen Brooks (1983)
"The Last One to Know"	Reba McEntire (1987)
"I'm that Kind of Girl"	Patty Loveless (1991)
"Wrong Side of Memphis"	Trisha Yearwood (1992)
"Hey Cinderella"	Suzy Bogguss (1994)
"XXX's and OOO's"	Trisha Yearwood (1994)
"Wild Angels"	Martina McBride (1996)
"You Can Feel Bad"	Patty Loveless (1996)
"Strawberry Wine"*	Deana Carter (1996)
"We Danced Anyway"	Deana Carter (1996)
"Everybody Knows"	Trisha Yearwood (1997)

Top 40 Singles

"Baby Walk On"	Matraca Berg (1990)
"Things You Left Undone"	Matraca Berg (1990)
"Cry on the Shoulder of the Road"	Martina McBride (1996)
"Still Holding On"	Clint Black and Martina McBride (1997)
"Fool I'm a Woman"	Sara Evans (1999)
"If I Fall You're Going Down with Me"	Dixie Chicks (2001)
"You're Still Here"	Faith Hill (2003)
"On Your Way Home"	Patty Loveless (2003)
"I Don't Feel Like Loving You Today"*	Gretchen Wilson (2005)
"You and Tequila"*	Kenny Chesney and Grace Potter (2011)

* Received a Grammy nomination for Best Country Song.

They were a musical clan, gathering at her grandmother's house on summer evenings just as the gloaming crept down through the treetops. "They used to have wingdings on the porch and play bluegrass," Matraca says, "and it was just magical."

Her friend, best-selling novelist Lee Smith, observes: "For a real writer, everything depends upon who you're born to, and who raises you, and how you first hear language. In Matraca's case, it was the loving mountain voices of her mother and her aunts, and the beautiful music of the Kentucky hills they came from. Perhaps no child has ever been raised with music—literally surrounded by it—to the extent that Matraca was."

The harmonies of her mother and aunts naturally mimicked the slopes of their native Harlan County, rising and falling across the peaks and valleys of "In the Pines" and "Shady Grove." As their craggy undulations drifted off the porch, wandering down the mountainside toward the Cumberland River, the young Matraca must have felt a kinship to her ancestral ground, even in song. She laughs, remembering a visit to the nearby Hensley Settlement* when she rode 3,300 feet to the top of Brush Mountain in the back of a truck. "Uncle Charlie would get a six-pack of beer and just roar us up there."

Although she moves on in the conversation, speaking of other landmarks, that image of the young Matraca on her familial land high above the Cumberland lingers. It is an immediate likeness,

---

* Hensley Settlement sits on 500 acres of a soaring plateau that straddles Kentucky and Virginia. Founded by Sherman and Nicey Ann Hensley in 1903, it was the home of two extended families. At its peak, the settlement boasted 100 inhabitants who were self-sustaining and lived in relative isolation. They had primitive cabins and a one-room schoolhouse, and they fenced their farming and grazing land in elaborate split-rail patterns. The final resident departed in 1951, and Hensley Settlement is now part of Cumberland Gap National Park.

not aged by black-and-white or sepia tones. Her face and arms are as brown as biscuits, baked in the July sun. Her legs are scraped and bruised from climbing beech trees and playing in the creek.

She is alone, having purposefully wandered off from her sister and cousins. As she stands on that ridgeline, surrounded by cabins and fences built by her forebears, her precocious gaze makes it apparent that one's sense of place can also encompass a spiritual terrain, a geography of the heart that does not allow itself to be defined by a mere physical location.

Matraca runs her hand across the scaly, lichen-covered bark of a sourwood. She hears her uncle calling and dashes back to the truck. Back to Wallins Creek. And back to Nashville.

"I was always fascinated with music," Matraca says. "I knew it was what I was going to do. It's just one of those things—I always knew."

Her aspirations grew during a sojourn in Indianapolis, where her father took a job after graduating from Vanderbilt. Ron was a caring parent, teaching Matraca to play the piano. But Icie felt restless, homesick for Nashville's close proximity to the music world. Her pining took a toll on the marriage, and she and Ron eventually divorced. Icie returned to her beloved city, this time as a single mother with three children.

"We were really poor," Matraca says, explaining that her father was also strapped financially, paying off large student loans. And although Icie made some headway in Nashville—singing on several sessions, publishing seventeen songs, even briefly performing as a member of the Harden Trio—her career never flourished.

"Mom never got off the ground in the music business," Matraca explains. "She was too busy trying to survive. And it was difficult for women to be songwriters. It just never happened for her."

Icie enrolled in nursing school several years later, choosing to nurture Matraca's musical ambitions instead of her own. "She was very instrumental in teaching me how to write songs," Matraca notes. "She had a real natural ability. She didn't pursue it enough to really develop it, but she knew enough to show me what I was doing wrong."

She also made sure to expose her daughter to a community of musicians. "There were a lot more characters back then," Matraca says, "artists and crazy poets and redneck musicians. Her best friends are now Hall of Fame songwriters. I grew up around Red Lane ["Till I Get It Right,' 'Country Girl'] and Sonny Throckmorton ['Why Not Me,' 'Last Cheater's Waltz']. Those were my uncles. It was a great way to grow up."

Icie's coaching improved Matraca's songs and confidence, and they started visiting publishing companies on Music Row. Veteran songwriter Bobby Braddock—who helped pen such classics as "He Stopped Loving Her Today," "D-I-V-O-R-C-E," and "Golden Ring"—was so impressed that he offered to collaborate with Matraca. Their partnership produced "Faking Love," which was recorded by T. G. Sheppard and Karen Brooks and went to number one on 19 February 1983. Matraca was nineteen years old.

Nearly thirty years later, that day remains fresh in her memory: "My mother and I were driving along, and it came on the radio. We pulled over, and she had big tears in her eyes and was grinning from ear to ear. And she looked at me and said, 'How does it feel?'"

Matraca's voice turns ragged. "I would've given anything to give it to her." She allows a single tear to seep down her staunch cheek. It lingers on her chin for a second before she brushes it away. "Sorry," she breathes.

Icie savored her daughter's triumph, clutching her in her arms, along with the hope that it was an omen of more good days to come. A drive with her daughter. A song on the radio. A cure for her blues. Stability. Prosperity. Creativity.

The baby she had carried—the love child that had carried her to exile—had now fulfilled their joint dream.

Two years later, Icie was dead of cancer. She had celebrated her fortieth birthday that very week.

"It was heartbreaking," Matraca says. "I never had a real deep heart-to-heart discussion with her about what she wishes she would have done or what she tried to do and what happened and why it didn't happen. So that's kind of unfinished business in my life, and it will always be."

Matraca barely had time to contemplate these issues, though, as she quickly fell into the role of primary caregiver for her sister and brother, becoming "too responsible, too young," in the words of Lee Smith: "Matraca is deeply Appalachian in her devotion to her family. In fact, I don't think I have ever known anybody with such a strong ongoing commitment to her family—and this hasn't been easy."

After taking a couple of years to regroup and tend to her siblings, Matraca returned to the top of the charts in 1987 with Reba McEntire's version of "The Last One to Know." A string of successive cuts recorded by Randy Travis, Tanya Tucker, Marie Osmond, Highway 101, and Sweethearts of the Rodeo attracted the interest of Joe Galante at RCA Records.

"I was the accidental artist," she laughs. "I wasn't pursuing it very heavily, and everything that happened was like a dream. The irony is that I was twenty-six and they [the record company executives] were worried that I was too young. They were thinking, 'Well, we're pushing you as a singer-songwriter, but you haven't really lived enough to write anything deep.'" They revised their opinion when she played "Appalachian Rain," a haunting tribute to her mother:

Mountains of sorrow, mountains of pain
You'll never give for my baby a name

> My family's honor took it away
> Cry for your daughter, Appalachian rain

Recorded with background vocals by Emmylou Harris, the song became the emotional centerpiece of Matraca's first album, *Lying to the Moon*. It was released in 1990 and boasted two Top 40 singles: "Baby Walk On" and "The Things You Left Undone." She was nominated for Top New Female Vocalist by the Academy of Country Music the following year.

"I never would have thought that making a record would do so much for my writing career," she marvels now of *Lying to the Moon*. "It was huge. Trisha Yearwood had the record. Faith Hill had the record. Martina McBride had the record. Deana Carter had the record. All the girls that ended up recording my songs had the record."

Matraca found the leap from writing to performing difficult. She was now in the big leagues, opening for established acts such as Clint Black and the Nitty Gritty Dirt Band. "I wasn't ready for any of it. I felt very awkward and out of my league. I was paddling as fast as I could, but I wasn't a very Nashville performer."

She was undeniably a Nashville songwriter, however, with "I'm that Kind of Girl" yielding a number-one hit for fellow Kentuckian Patty Loveless in 1991, and "Wrong Side of Memphis" topping the charts for Trisha Yearwood the following year. Despite this acclaim, the country music industry didn't quite know what to do with Matraca. The emergence of Garth Brooks in 1989 was a watershed moment for Nashville, one that redefined the culture of country music itself. Throughout the early 1990s, Brooks filled arenas with his sold-out concert tours, offering audiences rock theatrics that included elaborate pyrotechnics and himself hurtling from a trapdoor and soaring over the crowd on a harness. Although such spectacles undeniably broadened country music's fan base, they also began squeezing out more literary performers who had composed the genre's backbone. Perhaps it was no coincidence that Rosanne Cash—who had produced eleven number-one hits, twenty-one Top 40 country singles, and two gold albums during the 1980s—relocated to New York during this time.

Matraca, too, began to feel this realignment as a recording artist. "The country label didn't want me anymore," she recalls. A second album, titled *Bittersweet Surrender*, was shelved, and RCA transferred her to its New York label, insisting that she make a pop record. The result was *The Speed of Grace*, which performed poorly on the charts.

"It was frustrating because I really felt like I could make my version of a country triple A* record," she says. "I was young and listened to triple A radio, and I don't think a lot of those guys did. It became neither fish nor fowl, and it was just kind of an odd record."

Matraca had temporarily relocated to Los Angeles to record *The Speed of Grace*, and she was miserable. "I was staying in Santa Monica, and I had to drive to the Valley every day to go to the studio. I was sitting in the car in this endless traffic jam, and they had this NPR program called *Citybilly*. They played [Merle Haggard's] 'Big City,' and I started crying. Crying buckets. All I wanted to do was go back home."

Her chronic homesickness confined her to the writing desk:

Fire on the asphalt, LA freeway
Santa Ana windstorm, come blow me away

The words flowed as steady as the river of her ancestors, the muddy waters that connected past to present, mother to daughter, Wallins Creek to Nashville.

---

* Adult album alternative.

> Oh Cumberland, I'm a faithful son
> No matter where I run, I hear you calling me
> The Mississippi's wide and long, St. Paul to New Orleans
> But my heart's resting on your banks in Tennessee

"Sometimes when I write I'll just have a melody and I'll be 'singing in tongues,' blurting out whatever feels good, and it could be syllables and gibberish nonsense," she explains. "But 'Oh Cumberland' came out, and then I had to find the meaning afterwards."

She turned to a map of the Cumberland River for perspective, speechless when she saw that it linked Harlan County and Nashville. "I couldn't believe it," she shakes her head. "There is an element to songwriting that's magic and spirit. I do believe that that idea was to make me look at that map."

By putting her family and her personal journey in perspective, the process of writing "Oh Cumberland" reawakened her collective memory. She returned to Nashville, renewed by the knowledge that, like her forebears, she belonged on the banks of the Cumberland. Her marriage to Jeff Hanna of the Nitty Gritty Dirt Band in December 1993 further cemented her sense of place and sustained her during the aftermath of *The Speed of Grace*.

In an interview with *Country Standard Time* in 1998, Matraca observed: "It was a perception problem as far as the labels were concerned in Nashville. . . . After that, I was *persona non grata*. No one was willing to give me a record deal."

Ironically, she was never in greater demand as a songwriter. She had two more number-one hits in 1994: "Hey Cinderella," cowritten with and recorded by Suzy Bogguss, and "XXX's and OOO's," released by Trisha Yearwood. More chart toppers followed two years later, with Patty Loveless's cover of "You Can Feel Bad," Martina McBride's "Wild Angels," and what would become her most successful composition to date, Deana Carter's version of "Strawberry Wine."

A wistful waltz recalling a young girl's loss of virginity and innocence, "Strawberry Wine" resonated with country music listeners across the country. "It's a true story," Matraca laughs. "Every girl in town had passed on it. I'm really amazed at what [it] did. If you had told me that it was going to do that, I would have laughed in your face." "Strawberry Wine" earned a Grammy nomination for Best Country Song and was named Song of the Year by the Country Music Association in 1997, testimony that there was still a market for intelligent and accessible narrative-driven songs.

Lee Smith agrees, deeming Matraca "a born storyteller, through and through." She continues: "Many of her ballads—such as 'Alice in the Looking Glass,' 'Back When We Were Beautiful,' and 'Appalachian Rain'—actually contain entire novels. Her characters have the grit and grace to tell their own stories and sing their own songs."

Nearly all Matraca's characters are strong females, which she attributes to growing up around tough Harlan County women. "Are you kidding? That was everything!" she grins, launching into a tale about participating in the BBC documentary *Naked Nashville*. "They asked my aunt Sudie if she was a feminist, and she said, 'Well, you know, I reckon we must be. This is just how we've always been!'" Pride floods Matraca's face. "There are no blue bullets in my family. It's pink bullets. It's definitely a female tribe."

A sign catches her attention behind the bar. "I didn't know they sold wine in here!" She laughs, high and long, before getting back to business. "It's all about the chorus or an amazing hook that you cannot get out of your head, like 'Ode to Billie Joe.'" She belts the refrain—oblivious to Fido's customers ordering their espressos—in a voice every bit as textured and soulful as Bobbie Gentry's: "Billie Joe McAllister jumped off the Tallahatchie Bridge."

"There are about a thousand words in that song and there's this unbelievably complex story going underneath. So I think if there is a secret, that's what I've always been about—I want somebody to have a place to go back to, to keep the familiarity and their attention so they can hear the rest of the story."

The success of "Strawberry Wine" and relentless lobbying by Patty Loveless helped Matraca land another recording contract, this time with the upstart label Rising Tide. "It was incredibly freeing," she says of making her third album, *Sunday Morning to Saturday Night.* Produced by Emory Gordy Jr., the record was a return to form, a literate and radio-friendly collection featuring the lighthearted romp "Back in the Saddle" and the bittersweet ballad "Back When We Were Beautiful."

"Radio still didn't want to play me," she says, "but it kind of didn't matter at that point. I was getting so many songs cut, and the critical acclaim was awesome." The record also afforded Matraca an opportunity to work with her aunts, who provided background vocals as the Calloway Sisters and toured with her across the country. But just as *Sunday Morning to Saturday Night* was taking off, Rising Tide folded, and the record floundered in the absence of the muscle supplied by a marketing team. "I just stopped, you know. I didn't know what I wanted to do next, so I just kind of semiretired as an artist. I went back down to zero and stayed at home. Wrote songs."

Although her recent compositions have been recorded by a new generation of artists, such as Keith Urban, the Dixie Chicks, Gretchen Wilson, and Terri Clark, Matraca laments what passes for country music nowadays. "I don't know what this is. It sounds like jingles to me, like a strip-mall version of country. There's a certain kind of song they all want, and it's creatively frustrating. The focus is more on getting on the radio, fitting into a mold. It's very narrow now. We've lost an audience . . . because of that. We're catering to college kids and housewives."

She turns her eyes to the tabletop, touching the tip of a fork with her right index finger. "Every writer I talk to is extremely frustrated. We all feel like whores at this point."

Due in part to her discouragement, Matraca took several years before even considering a return to the recording studio. Then she did it in baby steps, laying down instrumental and vocal tracks unhurriedly, carving out recording time while tending to elderly family members and health issues. "I've been making this record for six years," she laughs.

The result is *The Dreaming Fields,* a stunning collection of songs, stark and wise, teeming with Matraca's trademark melancholy. "When you've been married or had a relationship for a certain amount of years, life takes on a slightly more sepia tone," she explains. "Things get complicated, and you go to some dark places to get to the other side. And then family members have addictions, and there are parents with dementia, and on and on and on. The songs that came out of that were completely different, and I knew I wanted them to be heard somehow. It wasn't even about me wanting to go out there and be in the spotlight again; it's just that these songs meant a lot to me."

It's a compliment to say that *The Dreaming Fields* will never be played by mainstream country radio. The songs are too intelligent, too literary, too beautiful—like "Silver and Glass," inspired by the tragic life of Anna Nicole Smith, in which Matraca's plaintive voice soars over a gritty guitar and her own mournful lyrics. "I got to be close with women who were really bright and funny, but whose whole lives were devoted to men and people who would

"These songs meant a lot to me," Matraca says of her latest album *The Dreaming Fields*. (Photo by Glen Rose)

use what they wanted physically," she says. "There was a parallel with Anna Nicole—fading beauties with substance abuse issues. It's so sad to watch." Her voice trails off, and she looks down at her tea. "What happens when you get older is horrifying. It killed

Marilyn Monroe. And didn't they say Jayne Mansfield had the IQ of a genius? There's this thing that happens when you're that young and beautiful. You just get swept along."

But if Berg laments such heartbreak in "Silver and Glass," she allows for a dose of revenge in a scorcher called "Your Husband's Cheating on Us," a classic narrative song in the vein of heroine Bobbie Gentry. Cowritten with legendary spitfire Marshall Chapman, the song is based on a short story by close friend and famed southern writer Jill McCorkle, in which a man's mistress teams up with his wife after they discover that he has yet another woman on the side.

Berg says she "can't count the ways" her songwriting has been inspired by writers like McCorkle and Smith, beginning when she read Smith's *Fair and Tender Ladies*. "It sounded like my grandmother talking, and she's from old Eastern Kentucky," she says. "There are these beautiful, heartbreaking stories from the holler that my mother came out of. It didn't occur to me to write about that stuff, and that put me on a completely different path in my writing."

The title track of the album shows off that influence, reading like a Willa Cather novel, with Matraca's evocative voice gliding over her gorgeous piano:

Oh the sun rolls down big as a miracle
Fades from the Midwest sky
And the corn and the trees wave in the breeze
As if to say goodbye

Other tracks—"If I Had Wings," "Racing the Angels," "Silver and Glass," "Oh Cumberland"—evoke themes of loss and longing and escape, all in a rural setting. *The Dreaming Fields* is a true album, belonging alongside Emmylou Harris's *Pieces of the Sky* and Kris Kristofferson's *The Silver Tongued Devil and I.*

Upon its release by the alt-country label Dualtone in May 2011, the record received glowing reviews from the *New York Times,* NPR's *All Things Considered,* and *Entertainment Weekly.* But perhaps the most succinct endorsement came from a fan's customer review on Amazon. Under the heading "the best living country songwriter," he revealed, "I [have] missed her recording . . . [this is] the best album I have heard so far this year."

The Dreaming Fields might not have happened, Matraca admits, if it hadn't been for friends like Nashville-based publicist and writer Holly Gleason and fellow singer-songwriters Gretchen Peters and Suzy Bogguss. "[They] drug me out kicking and screaming," she says. "We've been touring the UK on and off for a few years, and that's been enormously helpful. I didn't think anybody would care. I really didn't. We played Celtic Connections, and it was a huge audience, and it came my turn and somebody in the audience yelled, 'Back in the Saddle!' That was good. And then I got the courage to go back."

Matraca also collaborated with Chapman ("Betty's Bein' Bad") on several songs for *Good Ol' Girls,* a musical revue based on the work of Smith and McCorkle.* After being produced regionally, the show debuted off Broadway in February 2010.

Perhaps her biggest professional achievement, though, came when Matraca was inducted into the Nashville Songwriters Hall of Fame at age forty-four in 2008. It was her first year of eligibility, having met the requirement of publishing a song twenty-five years earlier.

"She is one of eleven female songwriters to be inducted (along with 152 men)," Chapman, her longtime friend and colleague, ex-

---

* *Good Ol' Girls* was written and adapted by Paul Ferguson, a professor at the University of North Carolina.

plains. "She's right there alongside songwriting heroines Dolly Parton, Loretta Lynn, Marijohn Wilkin, Cindy Walker, Tammy Wynette, and Felice Bryant."

Matraca shrugs off the praise. "It's just another one of those strange but wonderful things. It's just like having a hit at eighteen, like getting a record deal when you weren't looking for one and didn't really perform. I'm trying to enjoy it while it's happening instead of going, 'Oh my God, how did I get here and when are they going to find out I'm not ready for this?'"

After publishing nearly 400 songs and earning a dozen Broadcast Music Inc. (BMI) songwriting awards, Matraca's place among country music's greatest writers is assured. But it would be a grave mistake to assume that her influence ends at Music Row. Berg counts writers such as Smith, McCorkle, and Alice Randall as her friends, when in fact, they are her peers. Her songs are literature, transcending the musical form.

"Matraca is not only a poet of place but of the commonplace— of good times and hard times, too," Lee Smith says. "Even her most commercially successful cuts have deep, real roots in Appalachian soil. Mountain dirt, thin and hardscrabble. For her, *being* Appalachian is a choice, as it has become for many whose careers or marriages take them far beyond our sheltering—and confining—rim of hills."

Wallins Creek, nestled in those mountains, remains part of Matraca's life. She returns often to visit Granny Calloway, who is stalwart at the age of ninety-four. As she drives those mountain roads, her Volvo hugging the curves of Highway 119 above the Cumberland River, her mind must wander back to her headwaters, back to her mother, back to that Greyhound that bore her downstream to Nashville. She has become that river, "Oh Cumberland," that bloodstream:

A memory knee deep in salvation
That old muddy water that once washed her clean

Essential Tracks

"The Resurrection"
"The Dreaming Fields"
"Racing the Angels"
"Back When We Were Beautiful"
"A Cold Rainy Morning in London in June"

10

Cathy Rawlings

From the Wings

History is often portrayed as a linear subject, a chronological progression of dates and events leading up to the present. Other times, its themes take on an erratic, zigzag nature, bounding forward and backward and forward again, seemingly at will. But sometimes history comes full circle, providing an emotional and serendipitous arc to those who live it.

The morning of 28 October 2010 was one of those moments for the eager crowd of 300 strong gathered at the intersection of Elm Tree Lane and East Third Street in Lexington's East End neighborhood. As ten o'clock drew near, the audience could hardly be blamed for growing impatient. After all, it was an event that had been nearly fifty years in the making for the city's African American community: the rebirth of the historic Lyric Theatre.

The ceremonial speeches began at the appointed hour, with city officials and community leaders framed by the gleaming chrome of the marquee. Perched on the awning against the backdrop of yellow brick was one word, its letters bordered in neon lighting: LYRIC.

When the theater opened its doors in 1948, it became an instant cultural center for Lexington's black residents in the Jim

Crow era—a movie house of their own, where they were not relegated to the balcony or to separate restrooms bearing the sign "For Coloreds Only." Here at the spacious Lyric, with its elegant Art Deco lobby, they took in the baseball biopic *The Jackie Robinson Story* and the lusty musical *Carmen Jones,* starring Dorothy Dandridge and Harry Belafonte. The Lyric quickly became more than just a cinema, hosting concerts by legendary jazz, soul, and R&B performers including Duke Ellington, Sarah Vaughan, Ray Charles, and Ella Fitzgerald. But by 1963, business had slowed as Lexington's theaters became fully integrated, and the Lyric closed. The building was effectively abandoned, falling into a state of disrepair until the city government finally committed to its restoration more than forty years later.

The community feted the theater's reopening with an event-filled weekend that included a screening of Lena Horne's 1943 film *Stormy Weather,* an exhibit by folk artist La Von Van Williams Jr., and an opening-night gala featuring singers Miki Howard and Ben Sollee and acclaimed Kentucky poets Nikky Finney and Bianca Spriggs. Six weeks later, the restored Lyric hosted its first stage production, *The Duke, the Women, the Music,* a roots musical based on the female singers in Duke Ellington's legendary band. These remarkable, largely forgotten women were portrayed by members of the Agape Theatre Troupe, a nonprofit, all-volunteer group dedicated to preserving African American culture in the Bluegrass State and entertaining the public at large.

The Duke, the Women, the Music was the brainchild of troupe founder Cathy Rawlings, a local singer, actress, director, and playwright with a long-standing connection to the theater. "I remember going to the Lyric as a child," she recalls with a smile in her voice. "My older brother and sister would take [another] sister and I on Christmas Day. I just love that when I walk in that star in the lobby is still there. My aunt used to live on Third Street, adjacent to the Lyric. Just to see it lit up and to see people dressed up real fancy, it was just *wow*! With all the history, when I heard it was going to [reopen], it was my dream to be able to perform there, to bring it back to life like in the old days."

She watched nervously from the wings on opening night, scrutinizing the faces in the multiracial audience for their reaction. The production brought down the house, and by the time she bounded onstage to take a curtain call at the end of the evening, she was beaming with pride, overcome with emotion. It was a rare moment in the spotlight for this multitalented artist, who is more accustomed to directing from behind the scenes or singing in the back row of her church choir. But she paused to savor this moment, an appreciation of her commitment to historic preservation through music and the arts. After bowing to the crowd, she retreated to the wings, a smile still lighting her face.

Despite possessing a lush alto, Cathy doesn't claim to be much of a singer. She rarely sings lead, and when she does, she is often self-conscious, concerned that her vocals don't pack the heft of other performers' voices. Background and harmony vocals are her comfort zone, the place where she feels most at home, adding texture and bringing attention to the talents of someone else.

"I've always surrounded myself with people who can sing," she says with a throaty laugh. "I love to sing. Love it. I've just always been entertained by singing and performing. I'm not really a singer, [but] if anyone sings anything, I will find the harmony note."

Her passion for song is rooted in the sounds of the black church, in the soulful gospel music that forms some of her earliest childhood memories. "We were born and raised in the church," she says of herself and her six siblings. "Our faith was our peace." But Cathy's large family was unconventional when it came to worshipping, building their lives around not one but two churches

Cathy Rawlings. (Photo by Larry Neuzel)

due to a split allegiance between her parents. While her father was a longtime member of Evergreen Baptist, her mother preferred Antioch Baptist.

"We went to both churches," she explains. "My mom only had two dresses. She had a black dress and a lavender dress, and she would alternate so people wouldn't talk about her, wouldn't realize she was wearing the same dress—one Sunday to Antioch and one to Evergreen."

By the time Cathy was five years old, she was singing in the children's choir at Antioch, performing in Christmas plays, and offering the occasional special song. She flourished in the creative environment and looked forward to the stimulating practice sessions, which was a good thing for her, she says. "Once you start singing in church, you're in that choir. If you're a good singer or a worthy singer and drop out, I mean, that's almost like being stoned. That's almost like being the woman who committed adultery in the Bible." She shakes her head, launching into a perfect mimicry of a church elder. "'Child, if you don't use your gift, God'll take it away from you.' So that's frowned upon. That's a big-time no-no. A big-time no-no."

Music, along with her church and family life, provided a safe haven from the racial tensions of Lexington in the early 1960s. Although her school had been desegregated, Cathy found herself the object of prejudice among many of her classmates at Mary Todd Elementary in the neighborhood of Warrenton. "There were seven black kids that went to this all-white school," she recalls. "My first-grade teacher was Ms. Reynolds. I was the only black kid in the class. You know how you go to the trips with little kids and they pair everybody off? Well, nobody ever wanted to hold my hand, so I always had to walk with the teacher. I was called, you know, *nigger* so much I thought that was my name: my name's not Cathy; this must be my name. All that—it just shaped me and molded me and then, coming from school, from that environment, it was such a relief to relax at home and be around family. We had a loving home."

Her mother, she says, counteracted the discrimination she and her siblings faced by teaching them the Golden Rule and leading by example, forbidding the use of racial epithets directed at white people. "My mom protected us from all that," Cathy muses. "She knew the danger of it. We were taught that, basically, this is what it is, and this is what you can do to make your life better."

Like so many other African Americans living in the South during this time, the family turned to their faith for solace. Although she doesn't recollect their pastor being overtly political about civil rights in the vein of Dr. Martin Luther King Jr. or Dr. Ralph Abernathy, Cathy explains that the theology and culture of the church allowed her to put the struggle for racial equality in perspective.

"There is a different scene with the black church experience. If you've ever been in the midst of a black church service, it's very different. The life experience and the troubles are different between white America and black America." To illustrate her point, she naturally turns to music, quoting a few lines of contemporary gospel singer Kierra Sheard's barn burner "Done Did It" to illustrate her point:

Put food on my table
And clothes on my back
Said if he don't do nothing else
I know that he's able cause he's
Already done enough

"Those aren't typical lyrics in [white] church songs. A white friend of mine says the black church experience is therapeutic, to sing those songs. The writing in a lot of those gospel songs . . . ," Cathy pauses and searches for an explanation before choosing something simple but nonetheless spot-on: "it's just from the heart."

The choir at Lexington's Imani Missionary Baptist Church is revving up for worship, focusing on things above as the cry of the organ and dissonant blues riffs of the piano fill the large, modern sanctuary. The director gives Cathy the signal, and she strolls out in front. As they launch into the spiritual "I'm Glad," she closes her eyes and offers up a silent prayer. Satisfied, she takes the microphone and begins to recite a poem, "The Creation" by famed Harlem Renaissance poet James Weldon Johnson:

And God stepped out on space
And he looked around and said:
I'm lonely—
I'll make me a world.

Published in 1920 and written as a tribute to African American religious oratory, "The Creation" occupies a hallowed place in black American culture. In the poem, God seems to take on the style of a black preacher, walking around, emphasizing specific syllables and pausing for breath at particular points during the creation story. Cathy's recitation mirrors Johnson's intended syncopation, and people across the sanctuary are responding to her impassioned rendition, lifting their hands and interspersing her pauses with shouts of praise. By the time she comes to the part where God breathes life into man, "Like a mammy bending over her baby," many are in tears. Even with all her experience in music and on the stage, Cathy herself is overcome with emotion.

"I couldn't even hardly get through it," she recalls later. "I would practice at home. It's just hard to get through it without just breaking down, without just shouting and rejoicing, because God is real." She shakes her head as punctuation. "This is not a play. God is real."

At age fifty-three, Cathy has taken the teachings of her childhood to heart, choosing to remain in the church choir or risk forfeiting her musical talent. But there is really no danger of that, because she has taken her commitment to music and to the stage beyond the church doors by forming the Agape Theatre Troupe. Founded in 2000 as Imani's Family Life Center Theatre, the troupe's roots can be traced back to an experience Cathy had as an actress with the Actors Guild of Lexington, where she received three Raymond A. Smith Excellence in Theatre Awards—nicknamed Smitty Awards—for her performances in *Yellowman, The Old Settler,* and *The Vagina Monologues.*

"I had been in a production with the Actors Guild, and the shows that I was involved in were connected with the Roots and Heritage Festival—that's an African American festival that happens here in Lexington every year. The director at Actors Guild thought it was important to connect with the African American community. I think the first all-black production was in '96. I auditioned for that and got a part. Not many black people came to the show. They did another show, which I was in, and there was such a struggle to get black people to attend the show."

Disappointed by the small turnout by the African American community, Cathy began contemplating the group's apparent lack of connection to the theater arts. "I knew that a lot of black people in the area hadn't been exposed to theater. Then along came Tyler Perry [the writer and director of such popular films as *Diary of a Mad Black Woman* and the Madea series], which is not theater but entertainment—so a lot of black people think that's theater, but it's not. I was asked to do a play for a fund-raiser, and it had a great turnout. I found . . . that [for] 90 percent of the audience, that was their first time seeing a play. That's when I said, 'Wow—there's a need for it.'"

Enter the Agape Theatre Troupe. For talent, Cathy turned to the most creative place she knew: the church choir. Finding considerable dramatic talent in the choir's ranks, she then mounted a well-received production of *Flyin' West.* But she quickly found that her audiences wanted music. "That's what black people expect," she howls with infectious laughter. "If you're not singing, it's nothing."

Cathy turned to her extensive musical experience to write and direct plays with a spiritual message that incorporated the sounds of the black church: *Above My Head, Church, Roll On!* and *At the Crucifixion: A Play for the Easter Holiday.* But the troupe's watershed moment came with its September 2009 production of playwright Elizybeth Gregory Wilder's *Gee's Bend* at the Lexington Opera House. Set in the isolated hamlet of Gee's Bend, Alabama, and interspersed with haunting gospel songs, the play recounts the story of Sadie, a young mother who joins the Selma civil rights march in 1965, against her husband's express wishes. When she comes home beaten to a pulp, he locks her out of the house to teach her a lesson, leading her to realize that she can raise money for bus fare north and escape her life in the South by selling her hand-

The Business of Art

To the general public, being an artist often conjures romantic notions of a creative life unfettered by the demands of more traditional careers. The image of the songwriter, alone with her guitar and a legal pad, remains prevalent. However, a working artist must also be a businessperson, contemplating royalties and ticket sales, among other economic demands.

For Cathy, keeping the Agape Theatre Troupe on sound fiscal footing is a challenge. "We don't have a budget," she explains. "We just got our tax-exempt status. A lot of those arts grants that are available, we're not eligible for them. We're not old enough."

Like other community arts organizations, the troupe depends on corporate and charitable contributions. "So far, so good," says Cathy, whose primary focus has never been on financial gains. "That's our goal—to introduce people to the theater, to educate, to empower people through the pieces we do."

made quilts. The success of the one-night-only engagement—the 940-seat opera house was nearly sold out—sent a clear message to Cathy, she told the *Lexington Herald-Leader* the following year: "It told me that the community was ready for a mainstream African-American theater."

Next on the bill was Cathy's ambitious production of her original play *The Duke, the Women, the Music* at the restored Lyric Theatre in December 2010. Featuring the vocal talents of eight women in the roles of Ellington's female singers, the play was both entertaining and informative, with its swanky musical numbers and tales of the era's racism. The troupe followed that up with *Voices of Freedom,* a series of monologues adapted from the narratives of slaves living in the Lexington region in the eighteenth and nineteenth centuries. But the genius of *Voices of Freedom* was that Cathy made it a collaborative effort, inviting internationally known Kentucky poet Nikky Finney to read original poems onstage as part of the production. "Her voice brought a new meaning to the monologues," Cathy says, explaining that the addition of Finney's work posed an implicit question to the audience: "What does that tell you, from these monologues of actual slaves to Nikky's poetry? Has nothing really changed, and whose fault is it? It's not white people's fault."

With its combination of narratives, poems, and music, *Voices of Freedom* was, noted the *Lexington Herald-Leader,* "part gritty history lesson, part performing arts monument to ancestors, and part impromptu church service . . . the kind of brutal, difficult-to-watch details of history to which young generations should be exposed." And this was precisely her aim, Cathy says, mourning that young black Kentuckians seem to lack awareness of their cultural heritage.

"I like to empower and educate. I really do worry about our young people. I worry about black America because there's no family structure anymore, the black family is almost nonexistent, babies are having babies. Way back then it used to be Big Mama or Granny or Grandmama, someone in a household could hold a family together, and now Big Mama or Grandmama—she's in the nail shop with green extensions in her hair, getting ready to go out and party, so there's no one left to mold the black mind anymore. For the first time I'm working with some teenagers now, I'm doing a workshop for our summer camp. We're trying to keep them engaged, to pull them in a different direction, lead them elsewhere. But who knows what these kids go home to, who knows what they're facing? We have a goal to reach out, to help the young ones, to show them something other than a Beyoncé video. I love Beyoncé, but to show them something different—that's our goal."

Since 1989, the annual Roots and Heritage Festival has become a Lexington mainstay. The monthlong series of events, including art exhibits, literary readings, concerts, theater, stand-up comedy, and a variety of sporting activities, attracts thousands of people from throughout the region every September. Named one of the Top Twenty Events in the Southeast by the Southeast Tourism Society, the festival is capped by a heritage parade and three-day street fair in downtown Lexington.

In recent years, the Agape Theatre Troupe has become a cornerstone of the festival, and 2011 promises to be no different. The group is scheduled to perform *Sweatin' da Bluez—da Muzikle,* Cathy's musical adaptation of three Zora Neale Hurston stories. It is based on *Spunk: Three Tales by Zora Neale Hurston,* a play written by Kentucky native and Tony Award–winning director George C. Wolfe (*Angels in America: Millennium Approaches* and *Bring in da Noise/Bring in da Funk*). Busy with rehearsals and costume fittings, Cathy is in her element. "Zora had these stories," she starts, breaking into a wide grin. "I just love her folklore. There is a musical score that goes with it, but I didn't quite like that, so I ventured out and I put some blues with it—John Lee Hooker, Robert Johnson, Big Mama Thornton. It's another attempt to tell people about Zora, about John Lee Hooker, about the blues. Maybe if they can hear and see it onstage, they will go and do a little more research, take an interest in it."

Sweatin' da Bluez—da Muzikle promises to follow in the Agape tradition, being an intersection of roots music—gospel, blues, and jazz—and other creative genres. And once again, the show will be staged at the Lyric Theatre, a place that continues to mesmerize Cathy with its artistic heritage. She and her troupe of performers are now members of the pantheon of artists that have graced its stage, their eloquent dialogue and vocal pyrotechnics mingling with the stilled voices of Ella, Ray, and Sarah and the music of Duke—heady company, to be sure. But Cathy returns to lessons she learned from singing in the church choir to explain the appeal of her troupe: "You observe the singers who just sing and the ones with the life experience to back it up. I have experienced so many singers that have grown spiritually, and to sing of the goodness of God and what he has done for you and what he has brought you through—it's just unbelievable."

Essential Productions

Sweatin' da Bluez—da Muzikle
Gee's Bend
The Duke, the Women, the Music
Voices of Freedom
Flyin' West
A Song for Coretta
Crowns: A Gospel Musical
Memories of Life . . . Unchained Melodies
At the Crucifixion

11

Dale Ann Bradley

These Prisoning Hills

Deep within the Appalachian Sound Archives at Berea College lies a worn videocassette of a rare film. Shot with inferior quality film, the images appear faded and grainy on the thirteen-inch television—the swish of a frilly mauve dress that was probably a flashing salmon color in real life, the tip of a blurry cowboy hat from a singer performing on a rustic stage.

When it was released in 1966, *John Lair's Renfro Valley Barn Dance* made no splashes in Hollywood. Despite the movie poster boasting the tagline "It's the biggest singin', dancin', fiddlin' show that ever burst out of Renfro Valley!" the film was ten years past its prime, more at home in the string of country music revue flicks of the previous decade (think Ferlin Husky and June Carter in 1958's *Country Music Holiday*). But John Lair—the crotchety entrepreneur who created Renfro Valley in 1939 as a music center to rival Nashville, Chicago, and Cincinnati—was not interested in being on the cutting edge of cinema. This was, in many ways, an act of preservation, a thumb of the nose to the changing times.

Nearly fifty years later, Lair's Renfro Valley community has been modernized somewhat, adding a new barn for concerts, a re-created shopping village, and an RV park. The Kentucky Music Hall of Fame and Museum stands on an adjacent lot, housing memorabilia and exhibits devoted to artists such as Loretta Lynn, the Everly Brothers, and Lionel Hampton. Yet even in the midst of these recent accoutrements, an air of loneliness permeates this sweeping valley, wafting through the rows of kitschy shops and surrounding the old barn and its fabled stage.

Renfro Valley is a haunted place.

When Dale Ann Bradley takes the stage in the old barn on a Wednesday night, it is hard not to see the ghost of Lair and his revolving cast of performers, many of them Kentuckians, lurking in the wings: Red Foley, Martha Carson, Homer and Jethro, Whitey Ford. But the specter standing nearest to Dale Ann is the great Lily May Ledford, founder of the Coon Creek Girls, one of radio's first all-female string bands.

Dale Ann and her music are direct descendants of Ledford, both in sound and in name. Her career largely began, after all, when she was hired in 1991 as lead singer of the New Coon Creek Girls and signed to a five-year contract at the Renfro Valley Barn Dance. Since the group's dissolution in 1997, Dale Ann has recorded a string of critically acclaimed bluegrass albums and racked up four International Bluegrass Music Association (IBMA) Female Vocalist of the Year awards. And if that's not impressive enough, fellow Kentuckian and bluegrass legend Ricky Skaggs has proclaimed, "I think Dale Ann Bradley is an awesome singer. It's heart and soul with her."

Her latest album, a stirring set of songs titled *Somewhere South of Crazy,* is poised to continue that streak. "I've got to get away," Dale Ann declares in the title track, a carefree number cowritten with country music legend Pam Tillis, who also contributes a seamless harmony. She resumes that theme of wanderlust in "Leaving Kentucky," with lyrics that echo "Heritage," the

"I think Dale Ann Bradley is an awesome singer. It's heart and soul with her." —Ricky Skaggs (Photo courtesy of Compass Records)

magnum opus of the late, beloved poet James Still, and its oath, "I shall not leave these prisoning hills."

> The hardest thing she ever did
> Was leaving Kentucky
> Though the mountains were her prison
> They would always be her home

If you detect a backstory in these lines or in the slight quiver in Dale Ann's voice as she trills the word *home,* you would be right on the money. She has left her native state twice. And she has returned as many times.

When she moved as a young wife to Jacksonville, Florida, in the late 1980s, she had what she calls "a big old dose of culture shock, big time." She shakes her head and lets out a wide grin before taking a swig of stout coffee laced with cream. We are talking at a truck stop just off I-75 in Renfro Valley, and the diner is booming with truck drivers who have pulled off the road for hamburgers or fried chicken. The room grows loud as they move from booth to booth, slapping each other on the back, lighting their Marlboros, and catching up.

That move was the first time Dale Ann had been anywhere outside Kentucky, she confesses over the din. "I'd been to Lexington and Louisville, driving for a few hours." Another sip of coffee, and then a full-on, smoke-stained laugh. "I hadn't ever been to Jacksonville, Florida!"

Dale Ann's formative years were spent close to home: Williams Branch, a shadowy, three-forked holler in Bell County, a few miles from the Kentucky-Tennessee-Virginia state lines. "I believe it was pretty close to the same as when my grandmother was growing up in the same community," she says. "A few more vehicles, maybe a few more TVs. Wasn't any city water; we carried water. Very religious. Everybody was tied to each other."

As the daughter of a Primitive Baptist minister, Dale Ann's exposure to "things of the world" was limited. This "strict doctrine," as she terms it, limited her contact with music as well. Her family's faith did not permit musical instruments, even as part of their worship, she says. "We didn't even have shaped-note singing." As constricting as this was, she also credits it with honing her musical ear, teaching her to listen for harmony parts. "Even though a lot of their songs were very lamenting, from the way that it sounded without musical instruments," she reflects, "it did give me a sense of listening to the lyrics of the song and how it affected the soul. That's what came out in the voice. It taught me about singing with emotion."

But over time, the staunch religious boundaries of Dale Ann's family were slowly being redrawn, largely in response to her musical yearnings. Her great-uncle, who had moved to Detroit after

World War II to work at the Ford Motor Company, recognized her talent and would bring her musical gifts when he returned to visit. One that was especially significant was an eight-track player, along with tapes of Loretta Lynn's *Hymns* and Dolly Parton's *Blue Ridge Mountain Boy.*

"I just thought that was great," she smiles. "That was the first exposure to [secular] music that I had." When the tapes broke due to the strain of her continually playing them, Dale Ann's father would take the cassettes apart with a screwdriver, splicing the reel with Scotch tape.

She was given a guitar at age fourteen and began singing during the summers at the nearby Pine Mountain State Park as part of a trio with the local high school band director and his wife. Still, she admits, "it wasn't comfortable at home doing that," and her parents went back and forth over the suitability of their daughter's participation. "It was trial and error for a long time," she recalls. "It was just something they had to really search themselves for. But I was determined, and I wore them down. I wanted to do it more than anything in the world."

Her desire for a musical career on the road was so intense, she says, that after she graduated high school she had to take what she calls a "three-year sabbatical." Although she was playing regularly at local shows, she had little hope of expanding her trajectory. She got married, and she and her new husband took off for Jacksonville, where they had a son, John. But their marriage was already on the rocks, and when her husband, who was in the navy, was deployed, Dale Ann returned to Kentucky, and the couple quietly divorced.

Settling in Somerset, she soon found that she was miserable without her music and recorded a four-song demo at a small studio in Barbourville, Kentucky. She traveled to Nashville to pass the demo around, and on the way back, she dropped it off at the Renfro Valley offices. That same day she received a phone call from Glenn Pennington, the facility's then-owner and ex-husband of Lily May Ledford, asking her to be a guest performer that weekend.

"I was just floored," she admits, especially when Pennington offered her a regular slot on the Barn Dance. "I thought, that's going to suit me just fine." She was further elated when she was hired to replace the lead singer and guitar player for the New Coon Creek Girls, which had been reorganized by Lair in 1979. Yet despite all the ground that had been broken by Ledford and the original Coon Creek Girls, as well as latter-day artists Alison Krauss and Rhonda Vincent, Dale Ann was confronted by what is still largely a boys' club in the bluegrass industry.

Choosing Love over Judgment

Despite moving away from her restrictive religious upbringing, Dale Ann has retained a soft spot for traditional gospel music. In 2001 she released *Songs of Praise and Glory,* a poignant collection that includes the traditional "Palms of Victory" and the country classic "Clinging to a Saving Hand," which has been recorded by everyone from the Chuck Wagon Gang to Conway Twitty.

Dale Ann returned to the southern gospel wellspring three years later with *Send the Angels,* a record that quickly became a fan favorite. On "Nothing Can Hold Me Here," she sings of hope in death—"You don't have to cry for me / Don't sing no sad song"—over a rousing chorus of banjo, guitar, and fiddle. A gentle treatment of Dolly Parton's "The Master's Plan" is also a highlight of the album, showcasing Dale Ann's crystalline voice.

"I picked each of those songs because I felt like they were uplifting," she recalls. "I don't want something that's hitting people over the head. I just want to do songs that are hopeful, that would maybe make you walk in other people's shoes."

"There has been some proving to do," she admits. "You got to work extra hard. It has been a male-oriented business, same as country. That's just been in recent years that the promoters would be open to having more than one female [on the bill]."

She pauses for another gulp of coffee. A fan walks by and recognizes her; Dale Ann's face lights up, and she reaches out for his hand. "Good to see you! Good to see you again."

"How y'all doing?" he asks.

"Doing good, getting ready to go pick in a little bit," she hollers as he strides away, Styrofoam cup in hand.

"The experience I got from all my years at Renfro Valley, it's just—," she says, trailing off. "I can't tell you how it's benefited me. It's taught me what to do and what not to do. Taught me a lot about song expression, what an audience really wants and needs from an entertainer. Renfro Valley has been invaluable."

While writing songs for *Somewhere South of Crazy,* Dale Ann kept returning to the motif of travel, to the physical and spiritual journeys she has taken in her life. On the gentle ballad "Round and Round," she sings of her relationship with the highway—"I move along on a quilt of never ending gray"—that takes her away "from where I want to be."

Dale Ann began to dream of moving to Nashville when she was a young girl in the fourth grade. One day while poring over a geography book, she realized that the nearby Cumberland River also wound its way to Music City, USA. Circumstances, however, kept getting in the way: an ill-fated marriage, motherhood, caring for sick parents. But once she enrolled her son at Berea College, she decided it was time to make it happen.

On the heels of her breakthrough album *Catch Tomorrow,* Dale Ann moved to Nashville in the fall of 2007, arriving with her Ryder truck the same week as the IBMA awards ceremony, which she would be attending as a nominee for Female Vocalist of the Year. After a strenuous day of unloading furniture and unpacking, she panicked a few hours before the ceremony when she realized that her stage clothes were still in boxes. "It was awful!" she howls. "I was running around that part of Nashville trying to find something to put on. I hit Target and anything else that was open. I was shell-shocked. I did not choose the right clothes—let's put it that way!"

Dale Ann was also scheduled to present an award, and she made sure to limit her time at the podium, scurrying back to her seat. A few minutes later, she was summoned back to the stage when she was named Female Vocalist of the Year, beating out longtime bluegrass luminaries Alison Krauss, Rhonda Vincent, Claire Lynch, and Sonya Isaacs. "I was surprised to death," she laughs. And she was further astonished when she won the same award the next two consecutive years as well.

Catch Tomorrow, she says, "turned everything around." Newly signed to Compass Records, a label that boasts musical innovators Kevin Welch, Beth Nielsen Chapman, and the Waybacks among its artists, Dale Ann felt free to flex her creative muscles, recording original material alongside a few well-chosen covers. "The whole musical mix of the album was different," she observes, a point underscored by a review in *Pop Matters* that called it "near perfect . . . heart-rending, joyous, and kick-ass in equal measure."

One song that fell into the latter category was an original called "Run Rufus, Run," an edge-of-your-seat, Appalachian gothic tale about a moonshiner in Dale Ann's native Bell County. "It was a composite of stories," she grins. "That name, Rufus, was a mountain name if there ever was one. It's just about people doing what they have to do to make a living. And he ends up being a hero. That's what I want everyone in Bell County to understand."

The record was also special because it allowed her to connect musically with her father. Having long ago given up his wariness of her musical pursuits, he suggested that Dale Ann record a cover of Billy Joe Shaver's masterpiece "Live Forever" (a line from the song also gave the album its name). "That song had made an impact on him lyrically, I think. He helped me with my son and [had] been a supporter [of mine] once it all got rolling, but he'd never really specifically said anything about any particular song until then. I felt real compelled that if that song meant something to him, he had a reason why he wanted me to do it."

Considered by many critics, fans, and industry insiders to be the definitive version of "Live Forever," Dale Ann's arrangement lends it extra poignancy, with its lonesome mandolin and banjo underlining the sheer emotion of the lead vocal. She fully inhabits the song and its tender lyrics about mortality, and by the time the last verse comes around, reprising the first, Dale Ann is holding the listener's heartstrings in every note and vocal inflection. "You're gonna want to hold me," she nearly pleads, the subtle trill and slight elongation of the word *hold* flawless.

"That [song] would sum up my spirituality," she says quietly. When questioned about her faith journey and how it has progressed from her legalistic upbringing, she takes a moment to contemplate, choosing her words carefully. "It's not been cut and dry. It's been a developing one throughout the years, one that has taken a different form since I left Bell County."

I point out the strand of Tibetan Buddhist prayer beads that circles her wrist. "Christmas present from my son," she explains. "I feel the way I feel from experiences that have happened to me, that have happened to others. I hope that I have learned to walk in other people's shoes and that I have learned not to be judgmental and harsh. I believe in being kind and loving everybody, and if we

Dale Ann Bradley, Bluegrass Music Queen. (Photo courtesy of Compass Records)

all do that, that's probably the big picture. The big picture is what I look at now."

The title of her next album reflected that enlightened compassion: *Don't Turn Your Back*. Released in 2009, the record cemented her place in the upper echelons of bluegrass music, landing at number two on the bluegrass charts and remaining a presence there for an entire year. *Don't Turn Your Back* was lauded by *Billboard* as a progressive mix of traditional tunes—including the Carter Family's "Fifty Miles of Elbow Room" and a nod to her Renfro Valley roots with the traditional "Blue Eyed Boy," a favorite of Lily May Ledford's—and modern material, such as her versions of Fleetwood Mac's "Over My Head" and Tom Petty's "I Won't Back Down," featuring Dale Ann's "stunningly beautiful voice." But the review reserved special praise for her original songs, calling them "as strong as her choice of covers." "Music City Queen," cowritten with Louisa Branscomb, chronicles the perils of seeking stardom in Nashville. "Music City Queen, how much heartache have you seen?" it asks, Dale Ann's voice brimming with empathy for the main character's plight—and perhaps even for herself.

"The whole album was recorded at maybe the most transitional time of my life," she says. "I was down there, getting adjusted." But despite her best efforts, she found that her Nashville dream was leaving her increasingly unfulfilled. "It was a big change for me. I've been down there all my life—back and forth, back and forth—but I was a mountain girl, and it just proved how much of a mountain girl I was." So she returned to Kentucky, first settling in Mount Vernon near Renfro Valley, and then moving back to her native Bell County.

The light changes outside the window, and Dale Ann turns away for a moment, her strong Appalachian profile set against the backdrop of the first rise of the Cumberlands in the distance, across the parking lot of the diner and the barns of Renfro Valley. "You know, concrete and steel and a lot of traffic—it just didn't sit well with my soul. Putting it in perspective is what it has done for me. And I still go back there when I need to. But Kentucky calls."

The music of her native state continues to beckon and inspire Dale Ann—the drone of a bluegrass fiddle, the light flecks of a mandolin, the swirl of a banjo. *Somewhere South of Crazy* is certainly a Kentucky album in its lyrics, but also in its instrumentation, provided by bluegrass luminaries such as Sierra Hull, Stuart Duncan, and Alison Brown, Dale Ann's longtime producer.

Although offering a modern twist on the genre—she throws in a Celtic-flavored take on Seals and Croft's classic 1970s hit "Summer Breeze" for good measure—Dale Ann has ensured that the album remains grounded in its traditional roots from both Eastern and Western Kentucky. She offers a stirring rendition of the late Dottie Rambo's "New Shoes," about growing up in poverty in the coalfields of Western Kentucky. While recording *Somewhere South of Crazy,* however, she was haunted by a song made famous by another Kentuckian, the Father of Bluegrass himself. But unlike Bill Monroe's lilting version of "In Despair," Dale Ann's is hard driving, determined, kicked off by a forceful fiddle solo that is soon joined by a fierce banjo, a rhythm guitar, and her piercing vocal:

> You made me love you
> You made me want you
> And now I need you
> All the time

A gut-wrenching number about pining for an indifferent lover, Dale Ann's take on the song could just as easily be read as a chronicle of her feelings about Kentucky's hold on her spirit as well as her physical being, demanding that she live within its borders. But hers is not a romanticized view of the state—how could it be? She has been closely acquainted with its poverty, with its often inhibiting religious traditions, with its judgment.

And yet she returns, time and time again. "I'm glad that I was raised in Bell County in the mountains without access to a lot of things," she declares. "I don't believe that I would feel about music or a lot of things in general like I do now if I hadn't experienced the whole experience—the good things or the bad things. It gave me a keen sense of actually thinking for myself. It's made me appreciate things."

As the gloaming of the new spring slowly creeps down from the distant ridges, engulfing the famous barns in shadow, Dale Ann recalls a fortuitous meeting with Lily May Ledford shortly before she passed away from complications of lung cancer in 1985. Dale Ann was a nervous high school student, just beginning to discover her voice, when she heard Ledford's husky vocals and frenetic fiddle playing at a folk festival at Pine Mountain State Park. "I had heard my grandmother talk about the Coon Creek Girls when they could pick up Renfro Valley [on the radio]," she says. "I was mesmerized. One of the greatest storytellers I'd ever heard in my life. Had the audience in the palm of her hand. Knew every mountain fiddle tune there was."

Dale Ann instantly sensed a connection. "I understood her. [She] had a lot of the same background that I had. Music was restricted. Couldn't get her hands on an instrument, way up there in Pigeon Holler. For folk music in general, for what the heart and soul of that music is supposed to be about, she was one of the most consummate representations of that I had ever seen. She made you believe every word. The music was straight out of the heart of Kentucky, and you could feel that with her."

Dale Ann finishes her coffee, returning the thick mug to the table with barely a sound. She casts one last glance down the valley before rising to head out and get ready for her show. "She paved the way. The heritage and legacy are still there."

Essential Tracks

"Run Rufus, Run"
"Music City Queen"
"Round and Round"
"Live Forever"
"Somewhere South of Crazy"

12

Jim James

The Ghost of Jim James Past

Memorial Coliseum is electrified tonight, and it's not just from the guitars and keyboards and monitors that crowd the rectangular stage in the back of the basketball arena. No, there's a current in the air that everyone in the audience senses, a power surge from the 5,000-strong crowd gathered on the black tarpaulin–covered gym floor that pulses up the side steps and into the bleachers. Mostly University of Kentucky students, they are savoring the cool spring night in Lexington after a hard winter. And with finals only three weeks away, the end is in sight, and that fact alone calls for a celebration.

They are in awe of the charismatic man onstage singing into the microphone, and when he wraps up the song, they yell and throw their arms in the air, clapping furiously. He is one of them, they believe, someone who has walked in their shoes and speaks their language. And they are right. After a quick gulp of water, he points to his right, down the Avenue of Champions. "I worked over there at Fazoli's scraping shit off bread pans. I'd come home to Holmes Hall all covered in butter and grease and sit down in front of that four-track [recorder] and sing."

But that was before—before the hit records and appearances at Bonnaroo and Lollapalooza, before the Grammy nomina-

Jim James. (Photo by Matthew McCardwell)

tion and the listing in *Rolling Stone* as one of the "20 New Guitar Gods." That was the mid-1990s, a lifetime ago, when the man in the black polyester suit was a struggling UK art student named James Edward Olliges Jr. Now he is Jim James, and tonight he is here with his band My Morning Jacket.

The audience applauds wildly, and a stagehand slips out from the wings carrying a black cape and drapes it over Jim's shoulders. As he leans into the mike, left hand raised above the crowd, the cape's red silk lining shimmers under the stage lights. Part ringmaster, part Elizabethan actor, he flings his transformative tenor high into the rafters, higher than any of the glassy-eyed students in the audience. They are one with the music, bobbing their heads and moving their hips, swaying in place and mouthing the lyrics—"have you seen my smokin guns?"—channeling the hazy reverb of the electric guitar and steady high hat of the drums.

After a few more songs, Jim still can't get the image of his younger self out of his mind. Throughout the day, he has encountered the person he was fifteen years ago, living in the dorm and dreaming of jamming for a living. Looking down at his guitar, he offers a few words of advice: "If you pray hard enough and listen to those ghosts, they'll really help make your dreams come true." Then he laughs, almost to himself. "Lexington is a really, really fucked-up dimension."

Earlier that afternoon, Jim bounds off the stage, leaving the rest of the band to run through the sound check. They are flailing away at "I'm Amazed," a muscular rocker from their 2008 album *Evil Urges,* electric guitars and drums inhabiting the empty arena. Jim pauses to converse with a sound engineer, his mouth right up to the hipster's ear to be heard over the music. Then, with a grin and a quick pat on the back, we are off into the bowels of Memorial Coliseum, happening upon an open locker room that turns out to be the dressing room of Ben Sollee, who will be opening the show. Ben is not here yet, so we help ourselves to his couch and steal a couple of bottles of water from his stockpile.

"All I did when I lived here was dream," Jim explains, leaning back into the couch. "I worked at Subway for a year, and I worked at Fazoli's right down the street. I just walked around and dreamed and wrote songs. I'm trying to let the gods know or whoever that I'm really thankful 'cause this town, Lexington, was like one big dream for me."

One of his earliest performances, he says, was at an open-mike night at Common Grounds, a funky coffeehouse just a few blocks over on High Street. But the former art student admits that during his two-year stint at UK, "shit was cool, but it wasn't great." Instead of finding a nurturing, creative environment, Jim recalls that his professors were a rather narrow-minded lot, leery of anyone with an inventive, rebellious streak. "I was just dreaming of better things and of a better way, and so I really have some cosmic, ghostly connection with this town, because I still see the younger me walking around with his headphones on, [thinking], 'Fuck, if I can only not work at Fazoli's today and play!'" He tried to stick it out, but the songs beckoned, and in 1998 he returned to his native Louisville.

Back home, he formed My Morning Jacket with his cousin Johnny Quaid on guitar, Tom Blankenship on bass, and J. Glenn on drums. "The music scene in Louisville growing up was really harsh," he recalls. "I felt like all the popular bands were really stuck-up. It almost made me angry. I was like, 'Fuck you. I am going to do this. You're not going to tell me I'm not going to do this.'"

Jim set out to prove them wrong. The following year the fledgling band produced its first album, a sparse set of songs titled *The Tennessee Fire,* released on the indie label Darla Records. But it was their follow-up album *At Dawn* two years later that defined the band's sound, with Jim recording his ethereal vocals in a grain silo, drenching the album in reverb, and featuring keyboard player Danny Cash, who had joined the group in 2000. Glenn departed shortly thereafter, replaced on drums by Patrick Hallahan, Jim's best friend from childhood.

By this time, the band had become famous for its theatrical concerts, and with strong reviews for *At Dawn,* My Morning Jacket was signed in 2002 to the major label ATO Records, co-founded by Dave Matthews. *It Still Moves* was released the following year to widespread praise, earning an astounding 9.1 out of 10 rating from *Spin,* which observed that the band had moved "the still-smoking amps from their lightning-strike live show into the studio." Quaid and Cash departed in early 2004, with guitarist Carl Broemel and keyboardist Bo Koster joining in their stead.

A stable lineup finally in place, the band branched out on its fourth album, titled *Z,* in 2005, experimenting with synthesizers and reggae influences. The album wound up on many of the year's "Best Of" lists. By 2007, Jim was in such demand that he accepted a cameo in the avant-garde Bob Dylan musical biopic *I'm Not There,* directed by Academy Award–nominated director Todd Haynes (*Far from Heaven*), performing "Goin' to Acapulco" with indie rock band Calexico in the film. The following year saw the release of *Evil Urges* and its groove-inflected tracks, including "Highly Suspicious" and "I'm Amazed," as well as a four-hour marathon set at Bonnaroo that has since acquired legendary status. To cap off an already triumphant year, *Evil Urges* received a Grammy nomination for Best Alternative Music Album.

Despite his success and the satisfaction of proving his naysayers back in Lexington and Louisville wrong, Jim was growing creatively restless. Two side projects livened things up a bit for him in 2009. The first was the six-song EP *Tribute To,* featuring the songs of George Harrison, a longtime hero of Jim's, with haunting arrangements of "My Sweet Lord" and "All Things Must Pass." But rather than crediting the EP to Jim James, he chose to bill himself as Yim Yames, a move he explained in an interview with music journalist Jeffrey Lee Puckett of the *Louisville Courier-Journal.* "I feel like it's just a little bit funnier and a little bit weirder. And then some-body saw that there's a guy who, like, plays acoustic covers in bars in North Carolina or somewhere and was going by the name Jim James. So I was, like . . . I'm just going to change it to Yim Yames." Profits from the EP benefited the Woodstock Farm Animal Sanctu-ary in New York, headed by fellow Louisvillian Jenny Brown.

Jim's second side venture of 2009 was with his new group Monsters of Folk, a star-studded collaboration with Conor Oberst and Mike Mogis from Bright Eyes and M. Ward from She & Him. The group had loosely coalesced in 2004, when the guys began playing together backstage at shows and eventually onstage. But due to musical commitments involving their groups and solo ma-terial, they were unable to finish a full-length album until 2009. The eponymous record was released to critical acclaim later that year, peaking at number fifteen on the *Billboard* Hot 100 and number three on the Top Independent Albums chart.

"For me, music in life isn't inspiring enough," Jim explains of his creative drive, reclining on the couch. "I like to keep it fresh."

"The way I see it, rock 'n' roll is folk music," British rocker Robert Plant said years ago, and in many ways, his statement still holds true, especially for bands like My Morning Jacket. As the group's primary songwriter, Jim's music is distinctly folk, blending in-trospective lyrics with captivating melodies. In his song "I Will Be There When You Die," from the band's first album *The Ten-nessee Fire,* he name-checked his native state: "I was born in East Kentucky / Home of where the grass is dyed." But on the band's latest album, *Circuital,* Jim says that they have taken their celebra-tion of Kentucky to new heights, infusing the music itself with the sounds of their hometown.

"When I think about Kentucky and when I think about Lou-isville, we always joke that it's got really deep claws. Once its claws are into you—a lot of people don't leave. And I'm fortunate enough to be able to travel all over the world, and I've lived in different places and stuff, but there's part of me that needs Louisville, like I need to be there. There's just something that I can't even explain. Something spiritual."

Jim and his bandmates found this mystical quality of their hometown so profound that they attempted to capture its sound on *Circuital*. Recorded with producer Tucker Martine (known for his work with indie darlings Sufjan Stevens and the Decemberists) in a church gymnasium in Louisville, the record is intended to be a sonic feast, and it more than delivers the goods. Jim and company defy convention by kicking off *Circuital* with the album's longest tracks, a sure sign that the listener is in for something epic. The grimy synth line of "Victory Dance," the record's opener, drones along under Jim's ethereal vocals—"Baby, I'm flying up above / looking down on the tired earth"—which eventually transition into a full howl on "setting sun." Further into the record, he keeps things deliciously mellow on the golden-tinged "Wonderful (The Way I Feel)," with its sinuous acoustic guitar and seamless harmonies. The liner notes claim that the album was "recorded in heaven," and it's an entirely believable proposition, with its otherworldly, good-acid-trip sound.

It was more than 100 degrees inside the gymnasium when they recorded *Circuital,* and that mugginess seems to have crept into the songs; when Jim says that you can hear Louisville in the air of the record, he's not bullshitting. "We set up in a circle, and we brought in our tape machine and some mikes and amps and stuff. There were no computers. There was no air-conditioning. The record's very natural—you hear the humidity in the air. When we recorded we left the doors open, so you can hear the birds sometimes. You can really hear the air, I feel like. The sweat and humidity of Louisville is in there, and I think it would be completely different if it wasn't."

Making *Circuital* in Louisville paralleled a more personal homecoming of sorts for Jim. My Morning Jacket's previous album, *Evil Urges,* had been recorded in New York, where he lived for a good chunk of the year, in a studio with the most modern equipment and technology. Those influences can be heard in the record's songs, such as the vibrant "I'm Amazed" and "Thank You, Too." But after *Evil Urges* was released, Jim found himself pining for his native town and abandoned his part-time life in New York altogether. He has come full circle, a notion that is reflected in the title of the band's latest record.

"I really think it comes down to friends and family," he says of his return to Kentucky. "The claws are so deep. I've got friends I've known since fourth grade. My sisters are having kids and stuff, and I just want to be there to see all that, you know? I don't want to miss that. I have to miss enough of it as it is, because I'm gone a lot. I try to be there as much as I can."

As music from the band's sound check continues to bleed into the dressing room, Jim's expressions of hometown devotion sound like a spoken-word performance. He rhapsodizes about "the sun hitting the trees and the green grass" during childhood jaunts to Cherokee and Joe Creason parks, with their acres of fields and woodlands, from his home in the Hikes Point neighborhood.

When the subject of school comes up, he shudders at the thought of St. Martha Catholic School. "I wouldn't wish that on my own worst enemy," he laughs. Yet it was there, in the fourth grade, that he met Patrick Hallahan, My Morning Jacket's drummer. And even though his parents were not music aficionados, he admits that his mother's love of the pop and rock music of the 1960s and 1970s had a huge impact. But even more than those in-

Discography

Solo

Tribute To . . . (2009)

With My Morning Jacket

Studio

Circuital (2011)

Evil Urges (2008)

Z (2005)

It Still Moves (2003)

At Dawn (2001)

The Tennessee Fire (1999)

Live

Celebración de la Ciudad Natal (2009)

Live from Las Vegas—Exclusively at the Palms (2009)

Okonokos—Live Concert Film (2006)

Okonokos—Double Live Album (2006)

Acoustic Citsuoca (2004)

Demos and B-Sides

At Dawn/Tennessee Fire Demos Package (2007)

Chapter 1: The Sandworm Cometh: Early Recordings (2004)

Chapter 2: Learning: Early Recordings (2004)

EPs

iTunes Session (2011)

Sweatbees (2002)

Chocolate and Ice (2002)

Split (2002)

My Morning Jacket Does Xmas Fiasco Style (2000)

Heartbreakin Man (2000)

fluences, Jim credits his inspiration to another unlikely source: the Muppets. "Those are definitely my earliest memories," he grins, running a hand over his untamed mane of brown hair. "The Muppet band was so great."

For a man who has famously shied away from labeling his music, his intense love of the Muppets makes perfect sense: their music was largely unidentifiable, an intersection of a variety of genres. He continues on this theme, eventually relating it to his hometown's influence on My Morning Jacket's music. "Louisville is this island, I feel like, that a lot of people try to cast names on it and labels. Like a lot of people, when you're up in New York and people hear you're from Louisville, they're like, 'Oh, you're a southerner,' and we're like, 'Well, not really.' When you're down in the South, they're like, 'Y'all are Yanks,' and we're like, 'Not really.' And I feel like our band has always identified with that because we have never been anything, really. We're not quite hippie enough for the hippies and not cool enough for the coolies, so we exist on some place where people who hopefully don't label themselves can enjoy what we do."

This philosophy has become contagious in Kentucky's artistic community, and it was the cornerstone of Jim's collaboration with innovative cellist Ben Sollee and old-school crooner Daniel Martin Moore on their album *Dear Companion,* an acclaimed song cycle that centers on the landscape of Kentucky and the destructive practice of mountaintop removal mining. The experience of producing the album and working with Ben and Daniel was a significant one for Jim, who calls the pair his biggest inspirations among his fellow Kentucky artists. "I was just so moved by what they do," he says, "what they were trying to convey through this album and how they were trying to educate themselves about the cause, and then how they were trying to educate and inform me.

It was a thrill for me to see these two completely different forces that are Kentucky, and see them trying so hard to push for something so positive."

But don't let Jim's modesty fool you: he has been one of those forces as well, lending his time, talent, and name to save the mountains of Eastern Kentucky. In December 2009 he joined forces with Daniel and internationally beloved author Wendell Berry in a musical and literary evening to benefit the grassroots organization Kentuckians for the Commonwealth at Louisville's premier arts space, the 21C Museum and Hotel. After the release of *Dear Companion* the following year, Jim took to the road with Ben and Daniel as part of the Appalachian Voices Tour, a string of nine dates that kicked off with a raucous show at the Lexington Opera House and wound its way through the region to the Newport Folk Festival. More recently, he witnessed the devastation of mountaintop removal firsthand, touring mining sites in Eastern Kentucky by plane and on the ground and meeting with residents dealing with contaminated water and homes damaged from illegal blasting.

Jim chalks up the very existence of mountaintop removal to pure greed, which he views as modern America's Achilles' heel. "It's so simple. It's like greed, unfortunately, trumps love and care all the time. Not for all of us, obviously, but for so many people in this world because that's how you're brought up. You're not brought up to help your fellow man. You're brought up to beat him—to do better than him and make more money than him and advance farther than him at whatever cost, you know, just to get that dollar and get bigger and higher and higher and higher. So like with mountaintop removal, it's just a matter of people not giving a shit. They just don't care whose land they're destroying because they don't see it."

When he describes mountaintop removal to friends and fans who haven't heard of the issue, Jim makes a simple statement to which everyone can relate: "Imagine turning on your water and tons of waste pouring out. Imagine not being able to go to your home because it's buried by water and debris [from a sludge spill]."

He returns to the subject of *Dear Companion,* heaping praise on Ben and Daniel and referencing the trio's shared love of their native state. "We made the record in Kentucky and we're all from Kentucky. Worked with other musicians in Lexington to do other things on the record. It just felt really important."

Halfway through My Morning Jacket's set that night at Memorial Coliseum, I exit the stage pit and weave my way back to the arena's entrance, turning to face the rear of the audience. As Jim and the boys break into the opening riff of "Golden," featuring a guest spot by Ben Sollee on cello, the crowd lets out a colossal blast of approval. A college kid stands off to himself near the sound booth, head-banging and playing a mean air guitar along with the band. Just above the throng floats a swarm of rectangular lights—videophones in action, preserving clips of the show for immortalization later that night on YouTube.

One of the videos proves to be a standout. Shot a quarter of the way back from the right of the stage, it captures the experience of a My Morning Jacket show. And it is an *experience*—no other word will suffice. Gilded orbs of light hit the phone just right, lending the video a sepia-toned hue; the color of the music has become a physical presence. The footage is shaky as the videographer succumbs to the beat. It's an apt metaphor for many of the students, twenty-somethings and others of all ages in this audience who are struggling to forge their own destinies, wandering around the streets of Lexington and Louisville with their iPods and dreaming of escaping their low-wage jobs.

"Louisville—and Lexington, too—these are places where I feel like people have to fight harder for their own identities," Jim explains back in the dressing room. "People always say to us, 'When are you going to move to New York? When are you going to move to LA?' And it's like you don't have to do anything if you don't want to. You just got to try to make it your own way, and Louisville helped me do that."

He says the same from the stage, looking directly at the rows of students in front of him as the band launches into another song. Then he moves his guitar into position, lifting his eyes toward the rafters, and with a nod of thanks to the gods and ghosts, he surrenders to the rhythm once again.

Essential Tracks

"Golden"
"Smokin from Shootin"
"My Sweet Lord"
"Wonderful (The Way I Feel)"
"Goin' to Acapulco" (with Calexico)

13

Kate Larken

Far West

Of all the summer evenings that Kate Larken recollects from her childhood, one stands out in her mind just like it was yesterday. It was the early 1960s in Carlisle County, Kentucky, in the far western part of the state, just south of the confluence of the Mississippi and Ohio Rivers. All day long the heat had hung like a limp dress on a clothesline, and even at the gloaming there was no breeze, only the monotonous whir of heat bugs.

In the years before air-conditioning was widespread, families typically retreated to the porch at twilight, sometimes with a guitar, but always with a story. This evening, however, Kate's family took it one step further: they invited some friends over, packing a cluster of chairs out into the yard, along with some guitars and a couple of amplifiers. Before long, their farmland was teeming with swinging country rhythms and the flattened thirds, fifths, and sevenths of the blues.

"In a little while the phone rang," Kate laughs. "It was some neighbors way up over the hill behind us, at least a half mile as the crow flies, calling to see if the music they heard was coming from us. They knew we played all the time, and the acoustics must have been just right for the sound to travel that evening." Her mother confirmed that it was, in fact, their music, and the neighbors were so delighted that they proceeded to phone in requests throughout the evening. "I see now that it was a way of life in that place and time," she says. "If you wanted live music, you made it yourself."

Kate's musical odyssey began here on "the west coast of Kentucky," as she is known to half-jokingly refer to it before launching into a passionate treatise on why it should not be lumped in with *Western* Kentucky, a label usually identified with the town of Bowling Green and the surrounding counties. "True *West* Kentucky is bordered by three big rivers—the Mississippi on the west, the Ohio on the north, the Tennessee on the east. The whole region's a water land, defined by rivers and dams and lakes and creeks and ponds." Those waterways affect the land itself, she says, which is different from the rest of the state, distinguished by sandbars, rich bottomland, and red rock. And then there's the weather: "It usually gets Tennessee temperatures, but Arkansas and Missouri storms."

This distinction is key to understanding the region's music: a melding of traditional folk, transplanted by the railroads, and the gritty blues that washed ashore from the steamboats. "Halfway between Memphis and St. Louis, halfway between Chicago and New Orleans," she says. "I grew up in the dead center of Blues Alley."

With rolling hills and vast fields as her playground, Kate whiled away her days on the farm riding horses and wading in nearby Hurricane Creek. Music, it seems, was everywhere—at home on the farm, in the pews of Corinth Methodist Church, at the foot of her grandmother's spinet piano. Kate often talks about the impression the latter made, describing it as her "most personal music crossroads" in a foreword she contributed to an anthology of writings about music. She writes of "being a preschooler . . . with my ear pressed into the resounding wood near her [her grandmother's] knees, *feeling* more than hearing the music she played."

Surrounded by this creative environment, Kate says the music was "just waiting to come out my fingers." And so it did when she moved with her parents and younger sister to Anaheim, California, when she was seven years old. Bob and Eva Petrie were recent college graduates and had moved west to teach, but they were quickly struck with a terminal bout of homesickness. "My dad had left his musician buddies behind in Kentucky," she recalls, "but he loved to play and missed it so much that he taught me all he knew, seven chords, just so he'd have me as a little rhythm section." By the time the family returned to Carlisle County the following year, young Kate had already written her first song and was proficient enough to participate, albeit tentatively at first, in her father's jam sessions with his friends on her little blue Stratocaster pawnshop guitar. "I was playing with a lot of older local musicians that my dad knew, like Banty Hooper and Uncle Mark Tackett (the man who had taught my dad to play) and Everett Jordan," she says. "There were a couple of fiddlers around there, and we'd pick up a piano player here, an accordion player there at different times. But I was also listening to regional radio continuously, so I knew the contemporary sounds of my place, and that included the sounds that filtered in from adjacent places, such as Memphis and Chicago."

By the time she reached high school, Kate was spending her spare change on 45s and LPs by Creedence Clearwater Revival, Bobbie Gentry, and Booker T. and the MGs. She was so inspired by their music that she started a rock band, playing rollicking covers of "Proud Mary" and "Green Onions." And as a student coming of age in the late 1960s, she could not escape the social message contained in much of the era's music. It spoke to her burgeoning political consciousness, she says, and made her realize music's potential to effect change. She began to openly express her social beliefs and helped organize a student sit-in to oppose her high school's conservative dress code.

But then Kate's life shot out of orbit, deviating from her obvious trajectory as a developing artist. By the time she turned seventeen, she was married to a fellow classmate (to whom she now refers as "the Accidental Man"), and a baby followed shortly thereafter. While most of her friends were applying to college, she was warming bottles and changing diapers. Doomed from the beginning, the marriage nonetheless sputtered through eight years and another child before the couple separated in 1980 and divorced the following year. Kate finally made it to Murray State University as a twenty-five-year-old single mother with two children in tow.

"My life just didn't follow the predictable pattern," she says quietly. "I didn't go to college on time, didn't have a typical ex-

Kate Larken's Musical History

Singers and music aficionados alike are known for keeping extensive mental lists: musical firsts, best guitarists of all time, essential albums. Kate is no different, and like most, she needs little prompting to begin ticking through her lists.

"My mother gave me a little blue and white record player at a fairly young age," she recalls. "First record I remember having was a 78 of Bing Crosby; first album was Gene Autry's *Rudolph the Red Nosed Reindeer.* The first 45 single I ever bought with my own money was 'Susie Q,' that Creedence Clearwater Revival song."

Kate also remembers different periods of her life by the albums she listened to. "Judy Garland's *Judy at Carnegie Hall* got me through grad school," she explains, before launching into a discussion of Emmylou Harris's discography. Lately, Harris's *Hard Bargain* and Amos Lee's *Mission Bell* have been in constant rotation on her stereo. "Good stuff," she grins. "Good stuff."

perience when I did finally get there. Building a career in music during those prime years when most people do it was out of the question for me. I had to support my kids by myself. Most of my peers had the luxury of being consumed with pursuing whatever interested them, but I wasn't ever able to concentrate either time or talent on my art, though I longed to."

Yet in the midst of her regimented and constricted life, Kate still found time to listen to music, and the songs of John Prine, Guy Clark, and Mickey Newbury soothed her weary soul. When a rare bit of extra money presented itself in the form of a $300 income tax refund, she splurged on an acoustic guitar. Slowly— ever so slowly—she began to secretly hope that her fortunes would change.

After a seven-year stay in Paducah, followed by a year each in Bowling Green, Lexington, and Frankfort working as a teacher and later at the Kentucky Department of Education, Kate bade farewell to the Bluegrass State in 1991. By then, her older son was a senior in high school and her younger son was in junior high; both were rooted in Carlisle County and wanted to experience living with their father. Kate briefly settled in South Carolina before moving just across the border to Tryon, North Carolina, a small town in the Blue Ridge Mountains, where she worked as a newspaper editor and began to play music for a living. "In my thirties, I finally got two years to myself!" she cackles. "That was one of the best periods of my life because I was finally getting to be myself."

That included fully embracing her identity as a lesbian. The move to the Carolinas accelerated both her coming out and her creative processes, she says. "My entire identity, suppressed for so long by circumstance, expectation, and fate, began to take form fast. I really found myself while living there." Kate's music also experienced a coming out, she remembers, as the songs just seemed to be waiting for her to write them down on the page. Her life was finally back on track, and she quickly made up for lost years. She recorded a low-budget album, began playing live gigs, and was named one of the top three songwriters in the Carolinas. When she met a fellow artist and decided to trade the steep crags of North Carolina for the coalfields of Virginia, a long period of creative and connubial bliss followed.

From her home near the Kentucky-Virginia border, Kate embarked on the second leg of her artistic journey in Kentucky—this time in the eastern part of the state. She became a full-time working musician, making another record in Bristol, Virginia, and touring small venues across the country, "from the Black Hills to Key West." When she experienced a lull in gigs, she often worked on a contract-for-hire basis with Appalshop in nearby Whitesburg, savoring her commute to Kentucky through Pound Gap on the state line. "The shape of those hills fit my eyes better than any other landscape," she says. "I've been given the tag 'honorary hillbilly,' and I take that as high praise. I experienced the countryside, climbed the hills, hauled wood for the stove, learned new ways to pronounce old words. The voices in the coalfields were warm and familiar to my ear." Being a native flatlander, Kate could not help but compare the two cultures and was surprised at what she found. "The people, in spite of different country accents, are basically the same in West Kentucky and in Eastern Kentucky," she marvels. "They use a lot of the same colloquial language. When I realized that the Cumberland River had been a major migration route, it all made perfect sense. They are the same people; they just don't know it, most of them."

A primary difference between the regions, she found, is their musical cultures. "Musicians, writers, and filmmakers who focus on mountain arts have done a damned good job over the past fifty years defining and marketing Appalachia," she says. "Unfortunately, there has not been such a widespread cultural movement in West Kentucky. It's ironic, though, because one of the most famous mining songs of all time, 'Sixteen Tons' [written by Merle Travis], came from the state's western coalfields. That was the same Muhlenberg County area [where] John Prine's grandparents lived—he wrote his most beloved song, 'Paradise,' about that place. And Travis was both preserving and developing a Western Kentucky thumb-picking style. This is where the Everly Brothers are from, where Bill Monroe was born and raised. Yet when these songs or styles are identified as Kentucky music, uninformed listeners automatically attach them to the eastern coalfields, and that's simply because its culture is more well known and well marketed."

But the sounds of the Kentucky and Virginia coalfields began to seep into Kate's music and art. She collaborated with her partner on *Teddy's Piece,* a play based on the life of Teddy Triplett, a woman whose husband was killed in a West Virginia mining disaster during the 1950s. As the production's actor and musician, the two toured "far and wide," including a stint at the Actors Guild Theatre in Lexington, where audiences voted it best play of the season. One of the play's featured songs, "Muddy Water," became the title track of an album that Kate considers her most significant artistic venture. Recorded at Appalshop and released independently in 1995, *Muddy Water* was a gritty collection of original songs that merged the blues of her native West Kentucky with folk elements from her new home in the mountains, creating a rich slice of contemporary Americana. She unleashed her inner folkie on the gentle "Early Dark," written during a trip through Pound Gap, and the up-tempo "Soft Blue Shirt." But she let loose on the bluesy "Baby I Trust You" and joked that even in the heart

Kate Larken. (Photo by Richard X. Moore)

of Appalachia, she could not escape her first love: "Hell, even when I sing a mountain ballad, it somehow comes out sounding like the blues!"

Kate toured extensively behind *Muddy Water,* playing everywhere from large theaters and auditoriums to small coffeehouses and libraries. "After all those years, [I had finally] begun finding my way around in the lower echelons of the music biz. And after a couple of trips playing at the Bluebird [Café] in Nashville [a famous songwriters' performance space], where my songs were well received, I had an eye toward moving up a notch." But when financial difficulties—so familiar to working artists—became insurmountable, Kate laid her music aside and returned to teaching, retreating briefly to Paducah and finally to Louisville in 1998, returning to the banks of the Ohio River, coming full circle.

It is a balmy evening in Louisville, one of those easy summertime twilights when the world is as it should be. Here at Kate's home on a leafy street in St. Matthews, the mosquitoes are held at bay by the screened walls of the back porch. Fireflies twinkle on and off in the fenced yard, a visual metronome to the faint hum of crickets.

A group of friends has gathered on the tiled porch, trading stories and songs in between swigs of beer and bites of roasted almonds—*swarping*, her gang calls it, a country distortion of the word *swapping*. Kate is holding court at the moment, her kind face animated by a good yarn. She leaps up from her rocking chair, still holding her sweating bottle of Bud Select, and acts out a hilarious tale that originated at another such gathering. Her small audience is doubled over in stitches, and soon she gives up and joins in as well, letting rip an enormous belly laugh that rings out over the neighborhood.

"I'm glad our neighbors like us," she quips, reaching for her guitar, a gleaming Gibson L-200 specially designed by Emmylou Harris, one of Kate's musical idols. To add her own personal touch, she has affixed a clear sticker that reads, "This machine confronts prejudice and reveals its shame," an homage to the great Woody Guthrie and Pete Seeger. "What'll it be?" she asks. "'Free Bird!'" a smart-ass hollers. She rolls her eyes and flips him the bird.

"Why don't you do 'Trailer Park'?" someone else requests. "Okay, 'Trailer Park' it is," she says, reaching down the neck of the guitar to clamp her capo in place. She strums an opening chord and launches in, eyes closed for a split second as if to orient herself. The words begin to pour out in her rural Kentucky trill, and she fixes an intense gaze on her companions as she comes to the refrain: "Things were good here in the trailer park, baby, till you put us in your little book."

This is a Kate original, a biting account of an academic in disguise who has come to study the seemingly simple residents of a trailer park. As she ticks through stereotypical images of rural life—including Airstream trailers and drinking a Bud on the front porch—she combines them with the unexpected, portraying the residents as an intelligent group that watches PBS. By the last line, it is apparent where her loyalties lie: "Nobody cares about your little book." She shakes her Gibson with a mock sneer, flinging the reverberations out into the yard. "Take that!" she bellows, collapsing back into the rocking chair and reaching for her beer. Though perhaps a bit more rowdy, this get-together is not much different from those of her childhood.

The Louisville segment of Kate's Kentucky passage began in the late 1990s, a dark time in her life that made her question whether she would ever pick up a guitar again. After a traumatic breakup, "everything hurt too much to try again for a long time," she says. "It was lonesome in there without music, it really was. [But] I listened even when I could not play. Somehow I did get it back, though, because it is my real self."

Kate refers to her depression as "one of those invisibly productive dormant periods," and she eventually emerged from it with a renewed musical focus due in part to a supportive group of friends and a long-term romance with someone who allowed her the room to breathe as an artist. At the time, she was teaching school to make ends meet, but after a few years, she took a leap of faith and fulfilled a long-held dream of starting her own business, a textbook publishing company dubbed Eva Media. That venture was so successful that she soon established a literary imprint, MotesBooks, which has blossomed into a mainstay of regional literature. The transition to small business owner also allowed her more time for musical pursuits. "It's real freedom," she exclaims. "I follow the opportunities that reveal themselves, and I set my own work schedule, so I can easily balance music with that."

She returned to her activist roots by lending her voice to the fight against mountaintop removal mining, which is devastating Appalachia. In 2006 she contributed an original song, "Can't Put It Back," to *Songs for the Mountaintop,* a compilation album produced by Kentuckians for the Commonwealth that featured tunes from Kentucky musicians such as Jean Ritchie and the Reel World String Band. Following the record's release, she united with five other Kentucky writers and musicians (Silas House, Jessie Lynne Keltner, George Ella Lyon, Anne Shelby, and myself) to form Public Outcry, a band with a piss-and-vinegar sound that performed at rallies and toured college campuses throughout the region before it dissolved in 2009. A year later, Kate produced *Rising: A Gathering of Voices for New Power,* a cross-genre collection of songs, poetry, and prose to raise awareness about the issue. Her efforts to fuse activism and the arts were acknowledged when she received the prestigious Sallie Bingham Award from the Kentucky Foundation for Women in 2010.

After so much time and energy devoted to tackling mountaintop removal and other social issues, it is understandable that Kate is pessimistic about the current state of affairs in both the region and the country. "I did my part, and I did it the best I could, but I'm afraid that I and my compatriots were outnumbered," she says softly. "And now I'm older and getting to where I can't do as much as I used to, even though my heart is still young. It's really hard now to watch all of the good work that came out of my generation be subverted by greedy or judgmental special interests who have little regard or respect for all of humankind, for individual rights, for doing the right thing. I'm sorrowful about it."

These days, she is content to carry on her family tradition by making music on the porch or in a friend's living room, which she has done for the past several years with a raucous group of female musicians. "We have a great time, and when we get a groove going, it's like no other feeling in the world," she grins. "The music we play is diverse—from blues to folk to country to old time to rock to jazz to the occasional punk outbreak."

This is her true element, she says—swarping on a porch with her gang of friends, savoring a cool summer night, allowing the riffs and runs of her treasured Gibson to slip through the cracks in the stockade fence and into her neighbors' yards. There have been no complaints yet.

"My musicianship is all about joy and hardly at all about money," Kate explains. "If money is the only way to define a person's work, then I'm a failure. But if quality and variety and a wide range of experiences and growth as an artist define it, then I'm a hit. I do get paid to play, but I don't try to make my living at it anymore. I have 'aged out,' as they say. My time has come and gone. I was a small fry at it, anyhow."

At fifty-six years old, Kate might sound like she is throwing in the towel. But there is an interesting coda to her story: she has grown restless in Louisville, and after an amicable breakup, the road is beckoning once again. "Listen, I'm still a farm girl at heart," she says, peering over her glasses. "I've lived in cities much of my adult life, but if I don't get out of there pretty often, I go kind of nutty. I need to see trees and a horizon line that is made out of nature. The vagabond in me has always felt that tug."

This time, however, she is seeking solace outside her native state—maybe only for a spell; perhaps for good. She is heading far west. But when she crosses the Mississippi, Kate will not be leaving Kentucky behind. No, it will be traveling with her, lodged in her calloused fingertips, caught in the country twang and the river blues of her guitar.

"The gift and skill of music has been with me since I was seven years old," she says, "maybe since I was born. There is nothing else in my life, other than my parents, that I have had longer or more consistently. That's huge. Huge. Music is life, and it's lifelong. It's portable. It's patient, even when we're not."

Essential Tracks

"Muddy Water"
"Can't Put It Back"
"We All Live Downstream"
"So Ashamed" (with Sensible Shoes)
"Back to the Wall"

14

The Watson Twins

Southern Manners

"Nothing feels better than blood on blood," Bruce Springsteen sings in "Highway Patrolman," one of the great Americana songs of the last thirty years. But at the risk of tampering with one of the Boss's masterpieces, I would have to add that nothing *sounds* better either. Kentucky roots music has long known this to be true, a fact bolstered by the long line of family acts spanning both decade and genre: the lilting, birdlike trills of Jean Ritchie and her celebrated family; the high, calloused voices of Bill and Charlie Monroe, backed by the thrash of their mandolin and guitar; the rich, husky mother-daughter harmonies of the Judds.

But in the late 1950s and early 1960s, two boys from Muhlenberg County were sharing the sounds of Kentucky with the world, bringing their familial harmonies to pop hits like "All I Have to Do Is Dream" and "Bye, Bye Love." In 1958, at the height of their fame, the Everly Brothers released a roots-oriented album titled *Songs Our Daddy Taught Us,* featuring a moving cover of the old Louvin Brothers classic "Kentucky." With sentimental lyrics celebrating the state as "the dearest land outside of heaven to me," where "mother, dad and sweetheart all are waiting," it's a song that in all likelihood would never be written today—a portrait of a bygone era that produced more direct and maudlin lyrics.

Metaphor is the preferred songwriting technique these days, providing scenarios and symbolism that listeners can easily transfer to their own lives and experiences. But with this method comes a risk: when it is used poorly, the results can be tiresome at best, trite at worst. When it works, however, the product is often a thing of intoxicating beauty, a song that demands multiple listenings and musings.

Such is the music of Leigh and Chandra Watson. Better known as the Watson Twins, the Louisville-bred, Los Angeles–based identical siblings are swiftly becoming masters of the metaphor, "skilled in the art of harmony . . . their two voices . . . locked in a back-porch slow-dance," according to the *Los Angeles Times.* The sisters burst onto the music scene in 2006 when they lent their languid harmonies to indie goddess Jenny Lewis's *Rabbit Fur Coat,* easily one of the decade's finest albums, and released an eight-song EP of their own. With two critically acclaimed studio albums (2008's southern gothic *Fire Songs* and 2010's groove-inflected romp *Talking to You, Talking to Me*), they have steadily built up a national following, even wooing tough-as-nails *New York Times* music critic Jon Pareles in the process.

But it's one of their early songs that I keep returning to—the title track of their 2006 EP *Southern Manners.* The unvarnished ballad, written by Chandra, is about longing for the comfort and familiarity of a former lover. But if you read—and listen—between the lines, you might just find that the Watson Twins are singing about something else entirely.

> I can't tell you why I left you
> And I don't quite know why I'm here.

Los Angeles. November 1997. Leigh and Chandra Watson were fresh on the LA scene, having arrived from their home in suburban Louisville. The move was fortuitous, conceived in the af-

The Watson Twins. (Photo by Dan Monick)

termath of a six-month cross-country road trip following their graduation from the University of Evansville. They had returned to Louisville unsure of their next move, but with a vague plan. "We'd made a pact," Leigh says, before Chandra chimes in. "We were just like, 'We need to wait and see what the universe brings us. Whatever door opens, we're not going to ask any questions, we're just going to do it.'" Soon after, a friend from LA called and mentioned that he was in need of roommates. They signed up on the spot.

"We knew we wanted to experience something different," Leigh recalls of their move. They also had growing ambitions for their indie rock-flavored music, which they had begun honing in earnest in college. But LA added another layer to their style, one they had been hesitant to include back in Kentucky. Leigh continues, "My granddad would always say, 'When are you just going to quit singing those weird rock songs and sing country music?

That's where you're going to make any money.' And we were just like, 'No, this is what moves us,' and I think we were afraid to embrace that southern style of singing and writing until we moved to LA and it was something that people were interested in."

Leigh and Chandra both readily admit that they were hesitant to freely claim their Kentucky origins due to the widespread stereotypes and misconceptions about the state. Leigh tosses them out in shotgun succession with a sarcastic laugh: "Moonshine. The country bumpkin. The hillbilly. And married to your cousin. It's like, how many times have we heard that one?" But she also describes the mainstream culture's darker perceptions of Kentucky as a racist and homophobic place, and the need she felt to disassociate herself from those images. "I walked into a culture [in LA] where, in our neighborhood at that point, we were outnumbered by Hispanic people. We were also living in a very gay neighborhood. There were a lot of multicultural things happening, and for somebody to say, 'I'm from Kentucky,'" Leigh pauses and shakes her head. "We were nothing like the clichés. We didn't want people to go there."

Music and manners moved them to reevaluate their stance. Chandra tells the story of being introduced by a friend to a group of musicians at a bar one Saturday night, soon after the sisters' arrival in Los Angeles. At two in the morning, she announced on a whim that everyone was invited to brunch at their apartment around 10:30 or 11:00 A.M. "Our friend, before we left, he said, 'I don't mean to be mean to you guys, but they're not going to get up until four in the afternoon.'" Chandra was undeterred, however, waking early to cook, make coffee, and pick fresh flowers to create an inviting atmosphere. By 11:15, no one had showed except for their friend, who was busy apologizing for the others. "He's going through this whole spiel trying to make me feel better—[and] they all show up."

"One by one, they all showed up," Leigh picks up. "And they never missed another one of our brunches because they knew how awesome it was going to be."

Both say that this experience, of all things, helped clarify their personal identities as Kentuckians. "That was one of the positive things I felt I could bring here, you know?" Leigh says. "I could be proud to say 'I'm from Kentucky' because, yes—I do know how to throw a really great party. And I do know how to be nice to the ugliest, meanest person that exists because, you know what? I don't care to go to that level with you. And that has become who we are as people from Kentucky. People out here know that we have a fabulous Derby party. People know that we make music. People know that we go to the [merchandise] table and we talk to every single person who's in line. That's what we've chosen to take from Kentucky."

> But nothing has moved my spirit
> Since I saw you late last year

Louisville. Early 1990s. As teenagers, the burgeoning music scene in their hometown had an enormous impact on Leigh and Chandra. Rock bands like Slint and the Palace Brothers (Will Oldham's sobriquet; he is now known as Bonnie "Prince" Billy) were building Louisville's reputation as a destination city for cutting-edge alternative music. The girls began frequenting punk and hardcore venues such as Tooligan's on Bardstown Road, the Zodiac downtown, and the Machine, a St. Matthews laser-tag venue reincarnated as a music club.

"We were just gobbling up whatever kind of music we could get a hold of or be a part of," Leigh recalls. "A lot of times it would be at the community center or the veterans' [hall], you know, wherever the kids who were in the bands could find somebody to give them a room, and they'd bring in the PA and whatever else.

Everybody was in a band, everybody went and saw shows every week, and it was a really tight-knit sort of community, and everybody was supporting everybody else."

Chandra describes their exposure to this scene as a turning point in their art because they were encountering people around their own age who were creating provocative music and posters and screen prints. "I think that's where our music comes from. There is the indie rock, there is the rhythm and blues, there is soul music, there is rock music, and then there's also this underlying bluegrass, country, southern gospel kind of vibe to our stuff. At that young age, we were kind of soaking all these things in, and they eventually began, as we started writing, to come out."

By age sixteen, the twins were playing guitar and writing songs, which they took with them when they moved a couple of hours away to attend the University of Evansville. Chandra signed up as a theater major, while Leigh remained behind the scenes, painting in the art department. They still managed to stay connected to the scene in Louisville, Leigh says, traveling back and forth to catch live shows and hear friends play.

Their own music had progressed to such a point that, after graduating, they packed their bags and guitars and set out on the road for six months, camping and staying with friends and stopping to play at a few open mikes at coffeehouses in between. Both describe their venture as "a really eye-opening trip" during which they discussed their future as musicians. Cities such as New York, Chicago, and Seattle popped up in their conversations, but they ultimately decided to wait for a sign. It came from their friend in LA.

Every lover knows a reason
And every woman has felt the same
Although our minds record each heartache
A little lovin' can take away the pain

Los Angeles. Late 1990s. After a short stint living outside the city in the San Fernando Valley, Leigh and Chandra moved to the Silver Lake neighborhood, an eclectic, thriving arts district on the edge of Griffith Park, teeming with coffeehouses, clubs, and vintage shops. They quickly became fixtures on the music circuit, catching live shows, making friends in the community, eventually working up the courage to sign up for what Leigh calls "the *American Idol* of open mikes" at Highland Grounds, a neighborhood coffee shop. "They had their open mike every Thursday night, and you just signed up and *maybe* they called your name."

Leigh acknowledges that the experience was intimidating, but they persevered and were soon regulars at the weekly event, taking the stage with nothing but their acoustic guitars and taut sibling harmonies. The audience's response made the managers take note, and the sisters were soon being booked for their own shows, billed as Black Swan, after a haunting Nina Simone song that appears on her 1963 *At Carnegie Hall* live album.

Leigh and Chandra also began holding regular jam sessions with a musician from St. Louis named Brent Rowan. "He was Pentecostal, and so he had sung gospel music his whole life," Leigh explains. "The three of us singing together, we felt that spark of what all of us had felt as children, growing up in the Midwest and South and singing southern gospel music." The trio began performing live at venues around town, including Molly Malone's and the Coconut Teaser on the Sunset Strip, with Brent on lead and Leigh and Chandra singing backup vocals.

Their connection with Brent was just one of many they formed with other southern and midwestern expatriates, creating a kind of artistic community in exile based on mutual understanding. "We have a lot of friends from Kentucky who live out here," says Leigh. "They're our community and our touchstones. Those people call you on your bullshit."

By 2000, they were playing with a group of friends in a band named Slydell, honing a full-on blues rock sound. And although they found their burgeoning career frustrating at times, they ultimately found it rewarding as well. "That was a realization in coming out here, like that's where my heart is," Chandra says. "And this is a really hard profession to be in for a lot of reasons, but I think that our underlying connection with each other and with the music is what we continue to go back to. . . . We started doing this for a reason, and there's a reason that we can't stop doing it."

Hold me, hold me, hold me close
Caress my shoulders and my toes

Louisville. 1970s. Leigh and Chandra grew up in what they call a "conventional suburb" of Louisville, riding their bicycles and playing kickball. But their childhood itself was anything but orthodox. They were the creative children on the block, organizing a circus and recruiting other kids as performers. And then there were the costumes. "We decided we were going to build southern belle dresses," Leigh says. "So we straightened out all these hangers and we tied them onto belts and then draped sheets over them. We walked around for days thinking we were southern belles. But to us it was real." They giggle in unison at the memory, and Leigh adds, "I think my mom might have been watching the miniseries *North and South* at the time."

At the mention of their mother, huge grins light up both their faces. Like good southern girls, they give her credit for nearly everything. This includes raising them alone after the death of their father when they were still toddlers. They portray her as a woman years ahead of her time, "complaining about environmental issues ten years before anyone ever mentioned it on the news," Chandra says, even playing guitar and writing songs herself. But more than anything, she managed to establish a creative, freethinking environment where the twins were able to pursue a wide range of interests: ballet, gymnastics, horseback riding lessons. But it was music that struck the deepest chord, as the girls discovered their voices while singing in the choir at Southeast Christian Church, a nondenominational congregation in the area. That formal training was enhanced by the hours they spent delving into

An Excerpt from the Interview

JH: Real music fans should like their favorite artists to change and grow and try new stuff—how do you all stay fresh?

LW: That's important. We always try to come up with iTunes categories for our different records. It's like we're at a point in music where it's accessible, [where it's possible] to listen and find new music that's exciting and different and to be inspired by that music, and to be inspired by the things that are around you and that maybe you grew up with but you didn't know how to tap into. And I think that's where we're at with our music. And I think that's the hard thing for people to understand. [They might say], "We just want to hear them sing beautiful harmonies and country music or whatever," when we get excited about jazz or blues or even bossa nova.

CW: That'd be boring. I mean, after three records people would be like, "Oh, I know what they do." We would be bored ourselves.

LW: Yeah. You have to grow and evolve, and I think that's such an important thing for music in general. It's like if Elvis Presley never decided to—even in his later years, where he started experimenting—not that it was all great, but it—

JH: There was some great stuff.

LW: There was some great stuff, yeah. And it's like he couldn't sing "Jailhouse Rock" one more time.

their mother's eclectic record collection, which included albums from Cat Stevens, Emmylou Harris, Pink Floyd, and the B-52s. "We had more drive and ambition to do it [music] than we had for anything else," Leigh admits.

"Our mom always said [that] before we could really even talk, we would make these noises that was like we were singing together," says Chandra. "And then basically from the time we were little kids, we would get in so much trouble for singing at the dinner table because we would not eat. We would just sing. The whole dinner."

Their mother's friends were in a band together, and the twins remember creeping out of their bedrooms at night to sit on the stairs and listen to the practice sessions, which were often held in their basement. Unprompted, Leigh bursts into an a cappella version of Tommy Tutone's 1980s anthem "867-5309/Jenny" to illustrate: "Jenny, Jenny / who should I turn to? / 867-5309."

"We were fascinated by everything that was happening," she says after her impromptu performance. "Music was definitely present in our house."

"Around us all the time," Chandra agrees.

But the young girls were also surrounded by an extended family of fiercely independent women who were used to getting things done themselves, from gardening to installing garage door openers to fixing cars, according to Leigh. "They were always doing stuff, and it's like I didn't know anything besides women who just got it done and worked really hard to make things happen."

> Make me forget what I can
> Be my lover and my man

Los Angeles. June 2010. Dusk is descending across Silver Lake, seeping down from the mountains and through the banana trees and bougainvillea surrounding Leigh and Chandra's pool. A coyote howls in the distance, a wild resident of nearby Griffith Park. The twins are relaxing around a poolside table, chortling at the antics of Marty, their two-year-old cat, who has just attacked a palm tree with no warning. Their earthy laughs mingle and rebound off the side of their two-story stucco house, floating down to the street. Leigh's silky, dark hair gleams in the fading sunlight, pulled back from her angular face; Chandra's thick, curly mane looks like a halo, backlit to perfection.

"We're just riding the wave, man," Leigh says of their last decade spent making music, which began in 2000 with their five-year stint in the indie rock band Slydell. The group recorded three albums and played hundreds of shows in an intense period that both consider another college-like experience. "Someone asked, 'What was your aha moment [with music]?'" Leigh recalls. "And I think for me, when we moved out here I was working four jobs. I was waiting tables, I was working at a retail shop, babysitting people—like I was just doing a million things to pay the bills, and when we started working with this group of musicians, we didn't care how late it was. I'd go to rehearsal at eleven at night and rehearse until four in the morning or whatever and then go to work the next day. And I feel like that was a moment where I realized this is something I love so much that I'm willing to just run myself ragged and do everything possible in order to make it happen. It's the only thing that's keeping me going."

Both Leigh and Chandra admit to being plagued by moments of doubt during this time. "That doesn't go away," Chandra says, "because when you're an artist, you're continually creating. There's always doubt."

Leigh leans forward for emphasis. "We came from a really strong place, and our family is full of strong women who are like, 'You just pull up your bootstraps and you keep going.' And I think between that sort of thing that we came from, which was a background of people who were from the hills and hadn't lived easy lives and were definitely hard workers and didn't give up on things, to coming out here. . . ." She pauses, turning to look at her sister. "One of us would be feeling the doubt of like 'We should just go home,' [and] the other was going, 'No! Look at all these wonderful things that are happening.'"

"It would have been a lot harder for us had we not had each other," Chandra adds quietly.

When Slydell disbanded in 2005, Leigh and Chandra immediately picked up where they had left off with their own distinct sound, writing new songs and playing again as a duo. It had been years since they last performed as Black Swan, and both felt a change was in order. They initially rejected a band name centered on their own last name, feeling it labeled them as "country"—an association they were wary of due to what they considered the contrived pop music being passed off as country today. "It was lame," Chandra laughs. "[But] that was what everyone called us. 'Oh, have you met the Watson Twins? Oh, the Watson Twins sang on that.' And it's like, when do you start to realize you're just denying reality?" It didn't take them long to accept the inevitable.

The sisters had gained such a reputation that they were regularly asked to sing backup on session work. By 2006, they were in the studio themselves with former Slydell bandmate J. Soda, recording an EP of their own titled *Southern Manners* and planning sessions around their erratic work schedules. "It was like we graduated [college]," Leigh recalls, "and then all of a sudden we were releasing the Watson Twins' first record." But before they could even finish the record, they received another invitation they could not refuse. Jenny Lewis, the petite powerhouse behind the ass-kicking sound of indie band Rilo Kiley, invited the Watson Twins to lend their harmonies to her debut solo album, *Rabbit Fur Coat*. After a series of rehearsals, Leigh and Chandra recorded their vocals in one night, and Lewis was so stunned by the result that the album is credited to "Jenny Lewis with the Watson Twins." A hypnotic record combining elements of 1970s country and California rock, *Rabbit Fur Coat* was hailed as a masterpiece, causing music fans and critics to take note of the Watson Twins.

Southern Manners followed shortly, and soon Leigh and Chandra were touring the country both with Lewis and on their own as a duo, attracting the attention of legendary folk and jazz label Vanguard Records, with which they ultimately signed. Work on their first full-length album soon commenced, a roots-flavored set that Chandra describes as "southern Gothic meets Laurel Canyon." When *Fire Songs* was released in 2008, the *New York Times* featured the record as a critic's choice, observing, "the songs hold sorrow and longing, keeping self-pity in check with serene grace."

A live album followed, but for their return to the studio, the twins wanted to push the boundaries of their sound, incorporating elements of soul, blues, and even bossa nova. Leigh muses on this merging of genres at length, pointing to Emmylou Harris, Neko Case, and Cat Power as inspirations for the "consistent growth" in their work. "We're at a point now where there doesn't have to be one genre. There doesn't have to be country and jazz and rock and 'which iTunes category do you fit in?'"

Talking to You, Talking to Me, released in early 2010, was "a record that we wanted people to be able to move to," Chandra says. "They're going to be vibing out on it." The opening track, "Modern Man," set the mood, its rhythm section led by a sprightly high hat and subtle bass line. But its centerpiece was Chandra's ethereal lead vocals that effortlessly weaved their way through the spacious ambience of the song. Another standout was "Harpeth River," a husky blues number that would feel at home in a smoke-filled cabaret.

The following year, the twins merged the sounds of their pre-

"We're at a point now where there doesn't have to be one genre. There doesn't have to be country and jazz and rock and 'which iTunes category do you fit in?'" —Leigh Watson (Photo by Lauren Ward)

vious albums in *Night Covers,* a six-song EP. For this project, they chose songs that have inspired their own music, including a gritty rendition of Bill Withers's "Ain't No Sunshine" and a formidable reinvention of the Eurhythmics' "Here Comes the Rain Again" into a roots rock track.

Both Leigh and Chandra attribute their adventurous streak to their relationship as sisters and twins. "We're very connected as people," Leigh says, "like you would be to your best friend. And I think that connectedness has given us the freedom and encouragement to not be afraid to try new things and to be able to grow together. For us it's instinctual."

Well, I guess I owe you something too
Well, it seems you've finally come on through

Louisville. February 2010. On the eve of the debut of their second full-length studio album, *Talking to You, Talking to Me,* the Watson Twins decided to return home for a release party at ear X-tacy, Louisville's leading independent record store and, in many ways, the heart of the city's music scene (until it closed its doors in November 2011). But there was a problem. "We're flying in, and it's a freaking whiteout," Leigh moans. "There's already six inches of snow on the ground, and they're planning on thirteen more." The twins recall their dismay when they heard the growing list of road and bridge closings, followed by Mayor Jerry Abramson's plea for residents to stay indoors if at all possible. "We're just like, 'Oh my God. We're so screwed.' So we get to ear X-tacy, and one by one, almost 200 people showed up. It was awesome. It was a homecoming."

The store's longtime owner, John Timmons, expressed his appreciation to the Watson Twins behind the scenes, Leigh recalls. "He was just like, 'You guys don't know how much this means to me that you decided to basically pay money to come back here to play a free in-store.' And we were like, 'You don't understand that you're the reason that we know the music we do.'" She shakes her head, allowing the statement to sink in. "The first shows that I saw [were] at ear X-tacy when it was a shoebox down the street. We're grateful, and we just want to return the favor."

Timmons was emotional that afternoon, and three days later, all of Louisville learned why: the store was on the verge of closing. "The easy thing would be to turn the lights off and walk out next month," he said at a press conference in front of a capacity crowd that included Jim James of My Morning Jacket. "But this isn't my store, this is all of ours, and I will do everything to stay open. We don't want a handout or a bailout . . . we want your business." In spite of Timmons's appeal and a move to a building with cheaper rent down Bardstown Road, ear X-tacy ultimately caved to the financial pressures of a troubled economy and music fans' increasing affinity for digital tunes.

For their part, the Watson Twins see local independent record stores like ear X-tacy and WFPK, Louisville's public radio station, as community builders and a boon to indie musicians. But at the end of the day, it all comes down to music itself.

"There's so many people out here that when you say you're from Louisville, they're like, 'Oh my gosh, what a great music scene,'" says Chandra, before adding, "[Kentucky] is a little bit of everything."

Leigh smiles, nodding her head in agreement. "When you're in the middle of something, it's so hard to see what's around you. When we stepped away from it, we realized we had a really great, amazing upbringing that a lot of people don't get. And there's that melding of culture that happens here. You have those southern charms and that intellect from the North. You're in the middle of blues music and country music and even . . . midwestern swing. And then you've got jazz. It's like everything was reachable. It was all happening. For us musically, we couldn't have landed in a better spot."

> And my Southern manners do oblige
> Won't you come on over for a slice of pie?

Los Angeles. June 2010. The late spring evening has turned to night in Silver Lake, the electric glow of LA to the southwest obscured by dense thickets of trees that speckle the neighborhood. A chill has fallen, prompting Chandra to ask if we should move inside. We decide to stick it out, and she retrieves a bottle of Cabernet from the house.

Earlier in the evening, she described her song "Southern Manners" as a "love letter to Kentucky," an homage to the culture that shaped her and her sister's music. "Kentucky was the man I was talking about in the song. The lyrics are basically [saying] bring me back to what I know, which is this place that's treated me right, because I don't feel like I'm being treated right right now. It was a metaphor of a relationship. Every time I play it, it's Kentucky I'm talking about. It's a great love story."

That, at the end of the day, summarizes their relationship to Kentucky—a romance filled with joys and hurts and jealousies, but one that ultimately endures across the 2,000 miles that separate them.

As Chandra uncorks the bottle, Leigh talks about a group of their maternal ancestors who worked in vaudeville and of their great-grandfather, a fiddler named Smiley Dean. She named her song publishing company after him in tribute. "There is a piece of us that will always be there. You might live somewhere, but that's where you live, and you can live someplace, but your heart can be somewhere else."

Chandra nods and distributes the glasses, and we raise them instinctually. "Cheers to Kentucky," she announces, with a quick echo from Leigh. Their laughter rings out into the night like birdsong.

Essential Tracks

"Modern Man"
"How Am I to Be?"
"Harpeth River"
"Tell Me Why"
"Southern Manners"

Acknowledgments

Like so many good things in life, this book began over a cup of tea—with Laura Sutton, former editor at the University Press of Kentucky. Her encouragement, particularly in the earliest stages, was invaluable. Likewise, the patience, insight, and über-coolness of my editor Anne Dean Watkins made this project a joy. Many thanks also to acquisitions assistant Bailey Johnson, for her wonderful administrative skills; to the stellar marketing team of John Hussey, Cameron Ludwick, Amy Harris, and Mack McCormick; and to skilled editors David Cobb, Ashley Runyon, and Linda Lotz.

I am particularly indebted to the Anne Ray Charitable Trust, which generously funded a two-month fellowship at the Berea College Appalachian Sound Archives, as well as to the expertise of the college's archival staff: Harry Rice, Shannon Wilson, Jaime Bradley, Grace Sears, and John Bondurant. The Kentucky Arts Council kindly provided both an Individual Professional Development Grant and an Al Smith Individual Artist Fellowship. Ron Day, Judy Hensley, Le Datta Grimes, and Crystal Wilkinson were all quick to respond to specific research questions. Megan

Naseman and Jordyne Gunthert proved to be amazing transcriptionists. Ronald D Eller, Ron Pen, and Holly George-Warren read portions or all of the manuscript at various stages and offered constructive feedback.

Thanks to the artists who were unfailingly generous with their time, and to the managers and publicists who helped make our conversations happen: Alicia Brown, Lori Cloud, Kim Fowler, Connie Hunt, Drae Jackson, Lisa Klipsic, Laura McCorkindale, Jason Richardson, Jeffrey Smith, and Larry Strickland. Traci Thomas, Holly Gleason, and Marshall Chapman are good folk and fine raconteurs.

Finally, the bulk of my appreciation must go to my family, both blood and chosen. Silas House provided steady companionship and words of encouragement as I wrote and made sure I took proper dinner breaks. Ann and Harold Hayden have always claimed me as their own; Marcy Hayden and Garrison Minor are two of my heartstrings. Marianne Worthington supplied good feedback and even better company. Kathi Whitley was available whenever I needed a sounding board and help gathering contacts, and this book benefited from her guiding spirit. My old friend Josiah Akinyele provided lodging and taxi service in Los Angeles; Cyndi Williams and Kim Palmer offered insight, comfortable guest quarters, and the best bloody crumpets in NashVegas.

I'm a better person and writer for having known the late Mike Mullins and being a part of the literary family he built at the Hindman Settlement School's Appalachian Writers Workshop.

Special thanks to Alice Hale Adams, Adanma and Shane Barton, Chad Berry, Donavan Cain, Diane Dehoney, Connie May Fowler, Kevin Gardner, Sam Gleaves, Jan Goff, Jeanne Marie Hibberd, Jane Hicks, bell hooks, Ron Houchin, Maurice Manning, Greta McDonough, Karen Salyer McElmurray, Jennifer Miller,

Beth Newberry, Lisa Parker, Deborah Payne, Jackie Rogers, Amanda Runyon, Lee Smith, Lora Smith, Nick Smith, Erik Tuttle, and Neela Vaswani.

In memory of Melody Record Shop and ear X-tacy. Long live all independent record stores.

Bibliography

Berry, Chad. *The Hayloft Gang: The Story of the National Barn Dance.* Urbana: University of Illinois Press, 2008.

Blount, Roy, Jr. "Country's Angels." *Esquire* 87, no. 3 (March 1977).

Bogdanov, Vladimir. *All Music Guide to the Blues: The Definitive Guide to the Blues.* Montclair, NJ: Backbeat Books, 2003.

Bufwack, Mary A., and Robert K. Oermann. *Finding Her Voice: The Saga of Women in Country Music.* New York: Crown, 1993.

Clooney, Rosemary, and Joan Barthel. *Girl Singer: An Autobiography.* New York: Broadway, 2001.

Cohn, Lawrence, et al. *Nothing But the Blues: The Music and the Musicians.* New York: Abbeville Press, 1999.

Conway, Cecelia. *African Banjo Echoes in Appalachia.* Knoxville: University of Tennessee Press, 1995.

Garland, Jim. *Welcome the Traveler Home: Jim Garland's Story of the Kentucky Mountains.* Lexington: University Press of Kentucky, 1983.

Green, Archie. *Only a Miner: Studies in Recorded Coal-Mining Songs.* Urbana: University of Illinois Press, 1972.

Green, Douglas. *Country Roots: The Origins of Country Music.* New York: Hawthorn Books, 1976.

Hall, Tom T. *The Storyteller's Nashville.* New York: Doubleday, 1979.

Hay, Fred J. "Black Musicians in Appalachia: An Introduction to Affrilachian Music." *Black Music Research Journal* 23, no. 1–2 (2003).

Jones, Louis M. "Grandpa." *Everybody's Grandpa: Fifty Years behind the Mike.* Knoxville: University of Tennessee Press, 1984.

Jones, Loyal. *Radio's "Country Mountain Boy" Bradley Kincaid*. Berea, KY: Berea College Appalachian Center, 1980.

Judd, Naomi. *Love Can Build a Bridge*. New York: Villard Books, 1993.

Lange, Jeffrey J. *Smile When You Call Me a Hillbilly: Country Music's Struggle for Respectability, 1939–1954*. Athens: University of Georgia Press, 2004.

Ledford, Lily May. *Coon Creek Girl*. Berea, KY: Berea College Appalachian Center, 1980.

Lynn, Loretta, and Patsi Bale Cox. *Still Woman Enough: A Memoir*. New York: Hyperion, 2003.

Lynn, Loretta, and George Vecsey. *Coal Miner's Daughter*. Chicago: Henry Regnery, 1976.

Malone, Bill. *Country Music, U.S.A.* Austin: University of Texas Press, 1985.

———. *Don't Get above Your Raisin': Country Music and the Southern Working Class*. Urbana: University of Illinois Press, 2002.

Malone, Bill C., and David Stricklin. *Southern Music/American Music*. Lexington: University Press of Kentucky, 2003.

Miles, Emma Bell. "Some Real American Music." *Harper's Magazine,* June 1904.

Montell, William Lynwood. *Grassroots Music in the Upper Cumberland*. Knoxville: University of Tennessee Press, 2006.

Pearson, Barry Lee. "Appalachian Blues." *Black Music Research Journal* 23, no. 1–2 (2003).

Pecknold, Diane. *The Selling Sound: The Rise of the Country Music Industry*. Durham, NC: Duke University Press, 2007.

Raine, James Watt. Lecture notes. Berea College Appalachian Sound Archives.

———. "The Way of Life of the Mountain People of Appalachia." Unpublished. Berea College Appalachian Sound Archives.

Ritchie, Jean. *Folk Songs of the Southern Appalachians*. New York: Oak Publications, 1965.

———. *Singing Family of the Cumberlands*. Lexington: University Press of Kentucky, 1988.

Romalis, Shelly. *Pistol Packin' Mama: Aunt Molly Jackson and the Politics of Folksong*. Urbana: University of Illinois Press, 1999.

Sharp, Cecil. *English Folk Songs from the Southern Appalachians*. London: Oxford University Press, 1932.

Smith, Richard D. *Can't You Hear Me Callin': The Life of Bill Monroe, Father of Bluegrass.* Cambridge: Da Capo Press, 2001.

Wolfe, Charles K. *Kentucky Country: Folk and Country Music of Kentucky.* Lexington: University Press of Kentucky, 2009.

Wolfe, Charles K., and James E. Akenson. *The Women of Country Music: A Reader.* Lexington: University Press of Kentucky, 2003.

Index

Abernathy, Ralph, 172
Above My Head (play), 175
Abramson, Jerry, 232
Acoustic Guitar (magazine), 86
activism, 11–12, 38, 41, 50–55, 172, 201–3, 207–8, 215–16
Actors Guild of Lexington, 174, 211
Adkins, Trace, 69
African Americans: and church, 91–92, 96–97, 98, 99–100, 102, 169–71, 172–73; Blind Teddy Darby, 2, 10; Helen Humes, 2, 10, 15, 100; impact on Kentucky music, 8–9, 100, 137; influence on ballad singing, 5–6, 7–8; Lionel Hampton, 2, 10, 100, 180; Lyric Theatre and, 167–69, 178; Mose Rager and, 9; migration and music, 8–9, 55; as neglected area of scholarship, 2–3, 5–6, 7–8; racial integration and music, 6–7, 8–9, 55; Arnold Shultz, 8–9
Agape Theatre Troupe, 168, 169, 174–78; formation of, 174–75; Lyric Theatre and, 167–69, 176, 178; preserving African American culture, 168–69, 174, 176–

77, 178; productions of, 168, 169, 174–76, 177–78; success of, 174, 176; Cathy Rawlings and, 168–69, 174–78
Alabama (band), 32
All That Is Bitter and Sweet (Ashley Judd), 38
Alpert, Herb, 118, 148
Americana music, 16–17, 67, 70, 71, 108, 110, 211, 218; definition of, 1–3, 110–11; growth of, 16–17; inclusive nature of, 1, 2–3, 6–9, 16, 56, 57, 60, 110–11, 226; literary nature of, 63, 67–70, 72, 79, 81, 155–56, 156–58, 159–60, 161–64, 165; working class roots of, 9–13
Americana Music Festival and Conference, 16–17
American Idol, 37, 98, 224
Angels in America: Millennium Approaches, 177
Appalachian Voices, 41, 54
Appalachian Voices Tour (Sollee, Moore, and James), 54, 202
Appalshop, 85, 210, 211
Armstrong, Howard, 8
Armstrong, Louis, 98

243

Index

ences, 169, 171; Kentucky, influence of, 171–72, 176, 177; Lyric
Theatre and, 167–69, 176, 178;
musical influences, 169, 171, 172,
178; as playwright, 168, 175, 176,
177–78; on preserving African
American culture, 168–69, 174,
176–77, 178; productions, 168, 169,
174–76, 177–78; race in Kentucky
and, 171–72, 176; religious faith,
169, 171–72, 173, 178
Rawlings, David, 86
"Readin', Rightin', Rt. 23" (Dwight
Yoakam song), 128–29
Rebel Without a Cause (film), 120,
124
Redding, Otis, 111
Reece, Erik, 51
Reel World String Band, 12, 215
Relish (Joan Osborne album), 105–6,
112, 116
Renfro Valley Barn Dance, 14, 147,
179–80, 184, 185, 188, 189, 191
Riddle, Lesley, 7
Righteous Love (Joan Osborne al-
bum), 112
Rilo Kiley, 229
*Rising: A Gathering of Voices for New
Power* (various artists album), 215
Ritchie, Jean, 4, 11, 41, 49, 50, 53, 59,
81, 85, 215, 218
Roberts, Doc, 7, 10
Roberts, Elizabeth Maddox, 70
rock music, 1, 2, 3, 16, 70, 71, 114,
124, 125, 156, 192–204, 207, 216,
220, 222, 223, 225, 228, 230, 231
Rodgers, Jimmie, 6, 7, 50
Rogers, Kenny, 32, 35, 127
Rolling Stone, 106, 193
Rollins, Sonny, 100
Ronstadt, Linda, 125
Roosevelt, Eleanor, 14
Roots and Heritage Festival, 174, 177
roots music. *See* Americana music

Rowan, Brent, 224
Rowland, Kelly, 138–39
R. Prophet (Nappy Roots member),
136, 141
Rudolph the Red Nosed Reindeer
(Gene Autry album), 208
Rules of Travel (Rosanne Cash al-
bum), 17
Rural Radio (magazine), 10
Ryman Auditorium, 17

Saadiq, Raphael, 140
Seals and Croft, 189
Second Greatest Sex, The (film), 15
Seeger, Pete, 213
Sexton, Lee, 83–84
Sharp, Cecil, 4–6, 7
Shaver, Billy Joe, 187
She & Him, 197
Sheard, Kierra, 172
Shelby, Anne, 215
Shelley, Joan, 48
Sheppard, T. G., 154
Shine, Laura, 40
Short, Ron, 84
Shultz, Arnold, 9
Simone, Nina, 224
Singing Family of the Cumberlands
(Ritchie), 4
Skaggs, Ricky, 127, 180
Slaughter, Gustavus G., 63
Sling Blade (film), 123, 124
Slint, 222
Slydell, 225, 228, 229
Smith, Anna Nicole, 161–62
Smith, Bessie, 7
Smith, Jaclyn, 26
Smith, Lee, 21, 152, 159, 163, 165
Smith, Richard D., 9
Smith, Will, 133
Soda, J., 229
Sollee, Ben, 2, 40–46, 50–57, 60–
61, 168, 194, 201–3; bicycling
and, 45–46; cello and, 43–45;

Index

Index